Social Skills Activities

for Secondary Students with Special Needs

DARLENE MANNIX

Illustration by Tim Mannix

JOSSEY-BASS
A Wiley Imprint
www.josseybass.com

DEDICATION

This book is dedicated to Fred La Born, exceptional principal of F.W. Crichfield Elementary School and to all of the teachers and staff there who have educated my children.

Thank you!!

Copyright © 1998 by John Wiley & Sons, Inc. All rights reserved.

Published by Jossey-Bass
A Wiley Imprint
989 Market Street, San Francisco, CA 94103-1741   www.josseybass.com

Jossey-Bass books and products are available through most bookstores. To contact Jossey-Bass directly call our Customer Care Department within the U.S. at 800-956-7739, outside the U.S. at 317-572-3986 or fax 317-572-4002.

Jossey-Bass also publishes its books in a variety of electronic formats. Some content that appears in print may not be available in electronic books.

Library of Congress Cataloging-in-Publication Data
Mannix, Darlene.
    Social skills activities for secondary students with special needs / Darlene Mannix ;
    illustrations by Tim Mannix.
        p.   cm.
    ISBN 0-13-042906-6
        1. Handicapped teenagers—United States—Life skills guides. 2. Life skills—Study and
    teaching (Secondary)—United States. 3. Life skills—United States—Problems, exercises, etc.
    I. Mannix, Tim. II. Center for Applied Research in Education. III. Title.
    HV1569.3.Y68M363   1995
    371.91—dc20   95-12270

FIRST EDITION
PB Printing 10 9 8 7 6 5 4 3

About This Resource

Social Skills Activities for Secondary Students with Special Needs is a two-part curriculum for students at the secondary level who need to learn and then practice social skills. The first part, "Social Skills That Are Helpful and Necessary," is an intensive collection of lessons that focus on 20 basic social skills. The second part, "Social Skills in Action," consists of more general applications of these social skills to various settings, situations, or problems.

Part I

The first section of the book deals with the introduction and teaching of what each of the 20 selected social skills involves. Each social skill unit typically contains the following information:

1. **Rationale:** This is a brief commentary that suggests the importance and probable use of the social skill. This can be shared with the student.

2. **Student Worksheets:** Each social skill unit contains between five and seven ready-to-use student worksheets that introduce and elaborate upon each social skill. Answers, when applicable, are provided.

3. **Teacher Tips:** Since these units will most likely be organized and directed by a teacher, classroom applications are suggested. These may consist of simple suggestions, ideas, or specific plans for classroom use.

4. **Parent Pointers:** Difficulty with social skills is not limited to the classroom; many parents are also interested in hints that can carry over to the home setting. The teacher may wish to copy whatever suggestions may be helpful to parents and share them as needed. Parents who purchase the book will likewise be able to select what tips or ideas they feel will be most helpful to them.

5. **Practice Activities:** For each social skills unit, several activities are listed for teacher/parent consideration. It is important to know about a social skill; however, it is the use of that skill that is truly the goal for the student.

Part II

After students have completed the social skills training in Part I, they are ready to begin applying the skills to real-life situations. The material in this section is organized as follows.

Five different settings are considered: *home, school, work, among peers,* and *in the community.* For each setting, three levels of social involvement are presented: (1) routine situations—typical, "normal" situations that almost anyone would encounter; (2) problems or unusual situations—situations that are more complicated, involve problem solving, or are of a more atypical nature; and (3) enhancing the situation—opportunities to explore ways to create an excellent or more involved social life in the five areas.

Each of the five groups contains 15 free-standing worksheets; that is, any of the 75 worksheets could be selected and used for student application (assuming that the social skills have been taught and learned from Part I). They are in no particular order. Each is only one page in length and can be discussed in a single setting. While many of the worksheets require specific answers, most allow for open-ended student input and discussion. After all, everyone's particular situations are different!

How to Use These Materials

The social skills units of Part I are structured and can easily be teacher- or adult-directed. These activities could easily be incorporated into a group classroom setting (especially in a special-needs class). They could also be conducted in small groups. If a student is having particular difficulty with a certain social skill, it is possible that the student could intensely study that skill individually—with the hope that he or she would apply it quickly to a group setting.

When the student or class is ready to proceed to Part II, the materials are available for selection as needed. There is no particular sequence except for the progression of routine situations to problem situations and then expanded to include enhancing situations. Again, the use of the materials is dictated by the needs of the student(s).

Discussion is a crucial element of all facets of the lessons. Assuming that the lessons are conducted in some sort of group setting, students can share their insights and ideas with others in the group. The worksheets can serve as a vehicle for getting thoughts collected and as a starting point for a discussion.

Teachers may want to clarify their rules for conducting a group discussion before proceeding too quickly through the lessons. It should be decided who will lead the discussion, how students will participate (raise hand? jot down answers? go around in a circle with the opportunity to contribute?), and what types of comments are acceptable (criticism? put-downs? laughter?).

The most important outcome, of course, is that students learn and then internalize appropriate ways to behave around others. Being able to get along with others is a tremendously powerful tool. It is even more powerful (and rewarding) to know that one can control a situation by actively participating and contributing to the social outcome. That's what it's all about!

Darlene Mannix

About the Author

Darlene Mannix has been a teacher in public and private schools for the past nineteen years where she has worked with students of all ages who are at-risk, language disordered, and emotionally, mentally and learning disabled. She has also taught alternative education classes for middle school students.

Ms. Mannix holds a Bachelor of Science degree from Taylor University and Masters in Learning Disabilities from Indiana University. She is an active member of the Council for Exceptional Children.

She is the author of several resources published by The Center for Applied Research in Education, including *Oral Language Activities for Special Children* (1987), *Be a Better Student: Lessons and Worksheets for Teaching Behavior Management in Grades 4-9* (1989), *Life Skills Activities for Secondary Students with Special Needs* (1995), and *Self-Esteem Activities for Secondary Students with Special Needs* (1996).

Table of Contents

Part I

Helpful and Necessary Social Skills

Skill 1—Being a Good Listener

INSTRUCTOR PAGE

Rationale: Being able to listen to others is probably one of the most important social skills that an individual can acquire. It is through this mode that we learn a lot about the people we are dealing with, as well as obtain information we might find necessary. It is not always easy—in fact, it is often quite difficult!—to be quiet, to really listen to someone. But this is a skill well worth developing!

WORKSHEETS

Worksheet #1: Introduction to Good Listening

Answer Key:

1. talk; 2. important; 3. learn; 4. instructions

Worksheet #2: Skit: Identifying a Good Listener

Answer Key:

1. Alice

2. she responded to what Christine said, asked questions, gave Christine opportunities to continue to talk

3. ignored her comments, changed the subject, left the scene

4. problems about her sister and grandmother

5. let her get her feelings out, maybe do some problem solving about the car

Worksheet #3: How to Be a Good Listener

Answer Key:

1. c; 2. e; 3. a; 4. f; 5. c; 6. d

Worksheet #4: Important Listening Situations

Answer Key:

1. students can benefit from learning the short-cut; student should use eye contact, ask questions, give full attention

2. students can avoid making mistakes (perhaps costly), wasting time to have directions repeated; student should pay attention to instructions, use eye contact, ask questions

3. student needs to know any special needs that this situation may involve; student should ask questions, perhaps write down instructions

4. student should take care of the dog's problem before it gets worse; student should ask questions, pay attention to instructions

5. student is directly responsible for carrying out the play; student should use eye contact, pay close attention to the situation, don't interrupt

6. student's advice is being asked for; student should listen to details about the car, give full attention to situation

Worksheet #5: What Problems Do You See?

Answer Key:

1. listener is thinking about something else—won't get the list right; should give full attention to mother

2. listener is not giving eye contact to the teacher—won't get full benefit of the demonstration; should look carefully and listen attentively

3. listener is preoccupied with another task—won't realize what time to be home; should give dad eye contact and ask questions to clarify situation if necessary

4. listener did not pay attention to directions—probably got lost; should have asked questions, written instructions down, repeated instructions

5. listener is excited about car and not listening to warning—should give full attention to friend explaining about the car

6. listener is not using eye contact or hearing a thing her friend is saying—should give full attention to friend, make comments, ask questions

Worksheet #6: Skit Revisited: Identifying the Listening Skills

Answer Key:

Using eye contact, making sympathetic comments, asking questions about the situation, not letting Beth interrupt, giving full attention to Christine's comments

TEACHER TIPS

- When giving a lecture or going over key points, alert students to the importance of what is to follow. Teach them to pay attention when you start something with: "Now this is key! Pay attention!"

- Give students something to listen for prior to your lecture or comments, such as "Listen for these three points," or "Listen for the use of the vocabulary words," etc.

- Have students repeat your instructions. Find out if what you said is what they heard!

- Tell students not to be afraid to write things down to help them remember what they have listened to. No one can remember everything, even if it is selective!

PARENT POINTERS

- When giving instructions, keep it short and simple. Ask for confirmation of what your child thinks he or she is supposed to do.

- Sometimes a simple "Got it?" might be enough to cue your child to quickly focus on what he or she is supposed to remember.

- Don't forget to use eye contact. When passing between errands and household tasks, don't rush so much that you and your child miss the moment of actually connecting!

- Prove that you, too, are a good listener by repeating something important to your child that he or she mentioned earlier. Show that you noticed!

PRACTICE ACTIVITIES

. . . Ask the student to listen to a news report on the radio. Have him or her give a brief summary of the highlights.

. . . Have the student select someone whom he or she thinks is a good listener. This could be a friend, someone in the family, or perhaps a teacher or other adult. Ask the student to consciously spend time with this person observing what it is about that person that makes him or her a good listener.

. . . Challenge the student to spend one hour engaging in listening only; no talking! This means no interrupting, no commenting, and no body language that would indicate he or she is not listening. How hard is this to do for an hour? Why or why not?

Name_____ Date _____

Introduction to Good Listening

What are some things that you like to listen to? A favorite song or piece of music? A funny radio station disc jockey? A scary show on TV? The voice of your best friend on the telephone? The sound of your barking dog, welcoming you home? There are a lot of things we like to listen to.

One important social skill is that of being a good listener to other people. Maybe you would rather be a talker than a listener, and that is a good social skill, too. But it takes both skills to be a social success!

Why is it important to listen to other people? People often want to talk about what's on their mind. Maybe a friend has a problem. Maybe someone heard something that he or she can't stop thinking about. It really helps if a person knows that you will listen to them—especially if you don't tell everyone what that person wants kept secret.

It makes people feel important when you take the time to really listen to what they have to say. Think about how you feel when it's quiet when you are talking and you feel that what you say matters to someone. It's a great feeling.

Don't forget that you can learn a lot by being a good listener, too. Your teachers have a lot they want you to learn, and talking is one way they can teach you. But you have to listen to learn! You can also learn fun, interesting things about any topic you can imagine. Just listen.

Finally, remember to pay close attention when someone is giving you directions for how to do something. It's no fun to get lost in a strange city because you didn't listen to the directions, or lose everything you thought you saved on the computer because you *thought* the computer was just like your old one and you didn't listen to the instructions. Surprise!!

Why is it important to be a good listener?

1. People like to _____ about what's on their mind.

2. It makes others feel very _____ when you take the time to listen to them.

3. You can _____ a lot by listening to someone who has something to explain or teach you.

4. Listen very carefully when you are given directions or _____ for how to do something.

Worksheet #2

Identifying a Good Listener

Skit 1

Characters:	Alice, Beth, and Christine—three friends
Setting:	Walking down the hallway at school
Task:	Identify the good listener

ALICE: Hey, Christine, what's up?

BETH: Yeah, we haven't seen you around for awhile. Where are you hiding out?

CHRISTINE *(sadly):* Oh, well, you know I've been having some trouble with my sister. We have to share a room since my old, sick grandmother came to live with us. I lost my private bedroom—not that it was all that great anyway. But now I have to look at my sister all the time.

ALICE *(sympathetically):* Hey, that sounds like a real drag.

CHRISTINE: It is, in fact . . .

BETH: I can't stand my sister. I'll be so glad when she's off to college and I get the whole closet and her CAR! *(starts to cheer)*

ALICE *(concerned):* Is your grandmother pretty sick?

CHRISTINE: Yeah, she had a heart attack and was in the hospital—

BETH: My dad's always saying that he's going to have a heart attack one of these days if he doesn't quit smoking. *(pauses)* Do either of you have a cigarette?

ALICE: Beth! I thought you quit! *(turns back to Christine)* Will you be going to the game with us on Friday?

CHRISTINE: I'd like to, but it depends on if my dear sister needs the car.

BETH *(suddenly interested):* So you might not be able to drive?

CHRISTINE: Well, I don't know . . . my grandmother is—

BETH: Oh look! There's Paulina! Let's see what she's up to! Come on! *(takes Alice by the arm and pulls her away)*

Discussion Questions:

1. Who was the good listener?

2. Why?

3. How could you tell that Beth wasn't interested in listening to Christine?

4. What was on Christine's mind?

5. How could Alice's listening have helped Christine?

Name_____ Date _____

How to Be a Good Listener

Match the technique or tip on the left with an example on the right that shows a way to be a good listener.

_____ **1.** use eye contact

_____ **2.** make comments about the conversation

_____ **3.** ask questions

_____ **4.** repeat words that the speaker was using

_____ **5.** don't interrupt

_____ **6.** give your full attention to the speaker

Name_____ Date _____

Worksheet #4   # Important Listening Situations

Why is it important to be a good listener in the following situations? What tips or techniques could help you be a good listener?

1. The teacher is explaining a short-cut to solving some multiplication problems.

Why important _____

Listening tips _____

2. Your boss is demonstrating how to operate a new machine for frying French fries.

Why important _____

Listening tips _____

3. Your neighbor is going on vacation to Florida for two weeks and wants you to take care of his horses and chickens.

Why important _____

Listening tips _____

4. Spot has fleas! Your veterinarian is recommending a new product that will take care of the problem if you follow the directions carefully.

Why important _____

Listening tips _____

5. The football coach wants the ball thrown to *you* sometime during the game. The quarterback will call a special number that lets you know it's that play.

Why important _____

Listening tips _____

6. Your best friend is thinking about buying an old car that seems to be running pretty well, but he's not sure it's worth very much. He wants to know what you think.

Why important _____

Listening tips _____

Worksheet #5   # What Problems Do You See?

Why is the listener in each situation not doing a very good job? How could he or she improve the listening skill?

1. I want you to pick up a pound of hamburger, three bags of chips, and onion buns. Don't get the regular buns!

Yeah, yeah.

2. Watch carefully. I'll go through this step-by-step so you'll know how to develop this film.

3. Don't forget to be home at 7:00. It's a school night!

Does this piece fit here?

4. I thought you'd never get here! Didn't you turn right after the railroad tracks?

Turn right? Right? What railroad tracks?

5. Whatever you do, don't turn on the brights. They won't shut off.

I'm so excited about driving your car! Give me the keys!!

6. I got the worst haircut of my life at the mall. They over-charged me, too!

Do you like my new jeans? I got them at the mall. Oh, your hair's so cute!

Skit Revisited: Identifying the Listening Skills

Skit 2

Characters: Alice, Christine
Setting: School lunchroom
Task: Identify specific listening techniques

ALICE: Hey, Christine, how're you doing? May I sit with you?

CHRISTINE: Oh sure. Have a seat. Want a banana?

ALICE *(laughing):* No, thanks. Hey, you look kind of down. Everything OK?

CHRISTINE: Well . . . not really. It's just family stuff.

ALICE: I know family problems can really be tough. My parents went through a really bad time last year. It was rough.

CHRISTINE: Well, it's not my parents . . . *(waiting)*

ALICE: I remember you talking about your sister being a pain. Is that going any better?

CHRISTINE: Oh, I forgot I told you about her. Actually, she is the problem. We are unfortunate, unhappy roommates now that my grandmother is living with us.

ALICE: Is this a temporary situation?

CHRISTINE: Well, I guess my grandmother could die! *(laughs)* Oh, I don't really mean that. She's pretty sick.

BETH: Hi, guys! Wanna go with me to the gym? Hey—What's going on?

ALICE: Oh, we're having a discussion about families, I guess. Why don't we join up with you later? Is that okay with you, Christine?

CHRISTINE *(surprised):* Sure.

(Beth leaves)

CHRISTINE: It's not that I don't like my family . . .

ALICE: I know. All families have to readjust to things. It's too bad you have to share a room. Do you have to share your closet too?

(fading)

CHRISTINE: And the bathroom!! And our towels!!! And the phone!!!

What listening skills or techniques did you identify?

_____

_____

_____

_____

_____

Skill 2—Understanding Another's Point of View

INSTRUCTOR PAGE

Rationale: Understanding how someone else feels or what experiences that person has had can affect how that person reacts to situations as well as how you react to that person. By enlarging one's point of view to include how someone else might feel is one way to begin understanding another person.

WORKSHEETS

Worksheet #7: Introduction to a Different Viewpoint

Students are to read several paragraphs about why individuals may have different viewpoints on a given topic.

Answer Key:

1. time; 2. learn/experience; 3. why

Worksheet #8: Identifying Different Points of View

Students are to discuss possible reasons why individuals in the given situations may have formed different opinions.

Answer Key: (answers may vary)

1. the first man may live in Chicago; the second person may have played football in high school

2. the first boy appears to be studious and probably uses the encyclopedia a lot in his schoolwork; the girl may enjoy reading only for pleasure

3. the first person may have worked very hard in the history class and gotten good grades; the second person may have put little effort into the class

4. the first girl may have heard that comment about white cats; the boy obviously has an exception to that comment

5. the girl may have a distaste for mushrooms because of the way they look; the boy has a taste for them

Worksheet #9: What's the Basis for This Point of View?

Students are to identify why the characters on the worksheet have formed the basis for their opinions.

Answer Key: (answers may vary—allow students to defend their choices)

1. a; 2. c; 3. a, b; 4. d; 5. b, c; 6. a, d; 7. d; 8. a

Worksheet #10: Changing Your Situation, Changing Your Opinion

Students are to discuss how each character has changed his or her opinion after time or circumstances have affected the character.

Answer Key:

1. the man went from being rich to looking for a job to pay bills

2. the lady changed from distrusting foreigners to finding that they have become very good friends to her

3. the little girl grew into a big girl

4. the girl didn't agree with her mother's opinion, but years (and several children later) she did

Worksheet #11: What Are Your Opinions?

Students are to complete sentences with their first thoughts. Then, after giving each more thought, they are to consider how true their first opinions now seem to be.

Worksheet #12: Someone Who Disagrees With Me

Students are to record several of their strong opinions, then research someone whose opinion differs greatly. Through this project they will hopefully come to understand reasons why another person may feel differently about an issue than they do.

TEACHER TIPS

- As differences of opinion come up in class, take the moment to suggest students take a look at the "other side." How is it possible that someone else could feel differently?

- Plan simple debates within the class. Take a controversial issue (taxes, abortion, TV ratings, etc.) and have each student come up with both pros and cons for the situation.

- Ask students: "Do you think everyone agrees with you? Does that mean you are wrong? Does that mean you are right?" Discuss how numbers or majority may not have anything to do with right/wrong.

PARENT POINTERS

- You are a terrific influence on your child. Think about the impressions you give daily to him or her as you make comments about other people.

- Try to understand your child's point of view (even though it may be very different from your own). This, too, is setting a good example of at least exploring an opinion other than your own.

- Discuss how your family situation has changed over the years. Perhaps through job changes, moves, educational changes, family changes, now your situation is entirely different. Can you now identify more easily with the struggles of a single parent? A handicapped person? An elderly person? Talk about this within your family.

PRACTICE ACTIVITIES

. . . Assign each student to research the lifestyle of people from another culture. It is not only interesting, but eye-opening to find out how other people—who are very different from you—view life.

. . . Invite speakers to visit the class who have visited another country. Through slides, videos, and personal experiences, this may enlighten your students to realize that there are people in need all around the world.

. . . Follow a country in the news for several weeks. Track what is happening and try to work through what daily life experiences might contain for them.

. . . Obtain Pen-Pals from other parts of the country, particularly groups of students who are very different from those in your community. Find out what life is like for them.

. . . Assign students to do a book report on a political or historical figure about whom they have already formed an opinion. Ask them to report if their opinions have changed in any way after studying about the person in depth.

Worksheet #7 Introduction to a Different Viewpoint

Believe it or not, you may not always be right! Sometimes with a little more time, experience, and thinking things through, you might find that you want to change your mind.

Let's take a look at clothes. When you have a chance, look at some old photographs of your parents. If you can control your laughter, enjoy looking at the way they wore their hair and the types of clothes they wore. Back then, they would probably tell you they were extremely stylish! But now, people would only dress that way for fun or if they wanted to have a good laugh. Time often changes the way you look at things. Yet, there are still people who will insist that THAT way was the ONLY way to dress—and still is!

What about learning? Did you ever think that playing football was dumb or that science class is dull or that all cats are worthless? But what happened when you made the football team? It probably became a lot more interesting. And what about that science teacher who let your class loose in the back field to shoot off homemade rockets? Perhaps your opinion changed. And cats? Well, some people will never change their opinion about cats. But I know of someone who insisted he hated all animals but was recently sighted patting a kitten who had curled up on his shoulder and was purring loudly. It was through experience with these different ideas that people changed their minds.

Many of us form our points of view on things that don't make sense. We believe something because someone told us to. Or because you had one bad experience. Or perhaps because you didn't take the time to educate yourself about the subject. Take the time to think about WHY you believe what you do. You may find out that you're willing to change your mind with a little more thought.

© 1998 by John Wiley & Sons, Inc.

What are some reasons why people have trouble understanding another's point of view?

1. Some people have formed an opinion a long _____ go, and don't want to change.

2. After people _____ new things, they might agree that their original thinking was wrong—they just didn't realize it.

3. Another reason people stick to a point of view is because they don't even know _____ they believe what they do! It's easier to just say, "This is my opinion," than to give reasons why—even if it doesn't make sense!

Name_____ Date _____

Identifying Different Points of View

Each of the people in the situations below have a different point of view about the same topic. Why do you think these people feel the way they do?

1.
The Bulls are the greatest!! There is nobody who can touch Michael Jordan! Basketball is the best sport!!

If you want to see a good sports team, it's the Green Bay Packers, all the way. There's no better sport than football. It's America's game.

2.
I can sit and browse through the encyclopedia for hours. It's so interesting.

I can't wait to read the latest mystery novel by I.M. Scaree. I love to figure them out.

3.
Mrs. Cliff is such a fun teacher. She makes us work hard, but we have learned so much about history this year!

All Mrs. Cliff does is think of how many types of assignments she can give us. History is boring and pointless.

4.
Any cat that has blue eyes is deaf. I've had two like that. It's really weird.

This is Fluffy. Her eyes are as blue as the sky and she always comes when I rattle her bowl.

5.
I hate mushrooms. They are so ugly and disgusting.

I love mushrooms. Load them up on my pizza!

Name_____ Date _____

What's the Basis for
This Point of View?

These people have strong opinions or points of view about certain topics. On the line write the letter(s) of the reason(s) given that probably explains their point of view. Then decide how good of a reason it is.

a. experience with the situation
b. learning or knowledge
c. opinion that was heard from someone else
d. opinion based on a feeling

_____ **1.** "Girls are no good in math. The three lowest scores in my math class were girls."

_____ **2.** "My dad says that you should never buy a foreign car. They are nothing but trouble."

_____ **3.** "I stopped wearing my retainer before I was supposed to. Now I have to have more dental work done. I think I should have followed my dentist's orders."

_____ **4.** "I don't like snakes. I don't know why. I've never even touched one. But I don't want to touch one. I don't like them."

_____ **5.** "Violence on television is a really bad thing. It affects the way we think about killing and human life. I read an article that told all about the negative effects of too much violence."

_____ **6.** "I don't want to play on John's team. He's a terrible leader. No one can understand his directions and he yells at everybody who makes a mistake. I got so upset the last time we played, I just went home."

_____ **7.** I don't think there should be special parking spots for handicapped people. Handicapped people should just have somebody else do their errands. They drive too slowly anyway—they shouldn't be on the road at all."

_____ **8.** "If you go roller skating at Miller's Skate Park, be sure to bring your own skates. The ones I rented practically fell apart while I was skating!"

Name_____ Date _____

Changing Your Situation, Changing Your Opinion

Sometimes your situation can change drastically, which in turn might make you feel quite differently about that situation. How has that happened in each character's case below?

1985	1997

1.

I've got a new color TV, a Cadillac, and I'm going to Jamaica. I don't have time to worry about giving money to charity or poor people. I worked hard—they can, too.

Wow, I never thought that my business would fail. How can I pay off my debts? I have charged so much—I owe everyone. Will I be able to even find another job?

2.

I don't like foreign people. They just don't understand our ways.

Mr. and Mrs. Gomez are the nicest people I have ever met. She brings me soup every Wednesday. He has helped me repair my car so many times. I wish I had more neighbors like them.

3.

I hate boys. They are so ugly. All they care about is scaring girls!

I find boys rather interesting. In fact, oh, there goes one now!!!

4.

My mother said that living with an alcoholic is a nightmare. But I know that I'm stronger than she was. I can change my boyfriend's drinking habits!

Well, I guess his need for beer was more important than his need for me. Divorce time.

Name_____ Date _____

What Are Your Opinions?

Without taking too long to think, finish each sentence below. When you have finished, take time to think through WHY you completed each sentence the way you did. What reasons did you come up with? Which opinions do you think you might change?

1. School is _____

2. I can't wait to _____

3. My best friend _____

4. Turn the television on to _____

5. I hate to eat _____

6. I would give money to _____

7. Foreign people are _____

8. Girls are _____

9. It is important to _____

10. Computers make me _____

11. My favorite time of day is _____

12. Being popular is _____

13. People who kill other people should _____

14. Someone who is really pretty is _____

15. Someone who I'd like to get to know better is _____

Name_____ Date _____

Someone Who Disagrees with Me

Write two or three opinions you feel very strongly about.
(Politics, religion, and famous people are good starters!)

YES   NO

1. _____

2. _____

3. _____

    Now, select someone (real or historical, walking around in your school or walking around in Washington D.C., etc.) who has a very different—but equally strong—opinion about one of the topics you chose.

    Through interviewing, observation, and/or research, learn as much as you can about that person's viewpoint. Why does that person feel differently from you? What experiences may have contributed to that feeling? Even though you may still disagree, do you feel that you understand his or her position a bit more? Use the space below for your notes.

_____

_____

_____

_____

_____

_____

_____

_____

_____

_____

_____

_____

_____

_____

_____

_____

_____

_____

_____

Skill 3—Being Able to Communicate

INSTRUCTOR PAGE

Rationale: It is important to tell others how we feel about things that are important to us. Silence gives a message, but it doesn't give much meaning. Messages of anger or defiance may express how someone feels, but are not productive. By helping students learn what communication is and how to appropriately express what they feel and think, we can help them more effectively give and receive messages to others.

WORKSHEETS

Worksheet #13: What Is Communication?

Students are to read the paragraphs about communication and complete sentences summarizing the content.

Answer Key:

1. giving, receiving; 2. think, ideas, feel; 3. expressions; 4. messages; 5. spoken, no

Worksheet #14: Communication through Behavior

Students are to read the situations and decide what message is being communicated.

Answer Key:

1. Laurie knows (or thinks she knows) the answers to the math problems.

2. Tom is bored at the game.

3. Karla is really interested in painting.

4. Jeff does not like the cat around him.

5. Darla enjoys eating.

6. Susan's younger sister wants to imitate her.

7. Tom is frustrated with not being able to fix his motorcycle.

8. Benjamin enjoys spending time with Tony.

Worksheet #15: Communication through Expressions

Students are to match the message with the facial expression drawn on the worksheet.

Answer Key:

1. f; 2. b; 3. c; 4. d; 5. e; 6. a

Worksheet #16: Messages

Students are to read through comments that are given by characters on the worksheet and to decide what the message is.

Answer Key:

1. I'm proud of what a great athlete I am.

2. I say I don't like cheaters, but I'm going to cheat anyway.

3. I am an animal rights activist and pleased to tell you so.

4. It's really important to me that you win this game.

5. I know you are capable of better work.

6. I'm not interested in drugs.

Worksheet #17: Practice Your Communication Skills

Students are to work on some skits or role-playing to demonstrate how to communicate a message to various people.

Worksheet #18: Appropriate vs. Inappropriate Communication

Students are to read each situation and decide whether or not the way it is handled is appropriate or not.

Answer Key:

1. inappropriate—you could get caught and lose your job
2. inappropriate—you might try a less threatening approach first; but if that doesn't work, try more aggressive tactics
3. appropriate—try to break the mood of anger
4. appropriate—your grandmother will probably be happy that other people enjoyed her pie and will continue to bake them for you
5. appropriate—thanks are always appropriate!

TEACHER TIPS

- Use discussion of topics as a vehicle to allow students to communicate.
- Call on all students, especially the quiet ones. You may have to go gently at first, but expect all students to participate in some manner in your class discussions. There are "safe" ways of involving all students and having them express opinions ("Raise your hand if you agree with this," "Thumbs up if you think Bob is right, thumbs down if you agree with Renee.").
- Use journals as a way of getting students to communicate their thoughts.

PARENT POINTERS

- Keep the channels of communication open. This might mean do more listening than talking. But be as physically available as possible for your child in case the moment is right and he or she has something to say.
- Don't push if all you get is: "Whatever," or "Nothing happened at school today." Let your child know that you are interested in what he or she is doing, even if you have to do so indirectly by going to PTA meetings, showing up at school occasionally, volunteering for school-related events and projects, etc.
- Don't be afraid to say: "I might not understand, but I want to try. Will you give me a chance to try to understand what you are thinking about/doing?"

PRACTICE ACTIVITIES

. . . Invite the school counselor to talk to your students about the benefits of actually talking to someone. It can be very therapeutic and stress-relieving just to have someone identifiable who can listen and who wants to listen to what they have to say.

. . . Have students give short speeches (2 to 3 minutes) about something they feel strongly about. Be sure to ask them to give reasons for why they feel this way and to be as clear as possible about explaining these reasons.

. . . Select two students to sit side-by-side at a table with a board between them so they can't see what the other is doing. Instruct one to be the "leader" and draw a design (include shapes, colors, rotations of the paper, etc.). He or she must give directions to the "blind" partner on the other side. Afterwards, compare drawings. How well did the leader communicate?

. . . Have students cut out facial expressions (or even include interesting body language) and put a "speech bubble" with an appropriate phrase by the person. This can help them tune in to what the message might be based on the expression and body language.

. . . Tell each student you want him or her to give you (orally or in writing) ten sentences that begin with "I."

Name_____ Date _____

What Is Communication?

Communication involves giving and receiving a message. This message might be your thoughts about something (that you think Gino's Pizza is too expensive for what you get), your ideas (you come up with a great way to decorate the school hallway for homecoming), or your feelings (how angry you get when your brother teases you about your voice).

You might be giving a message to someone even if you aren't doing it intentionally. If you forgot to take the trash out (like your father asked you to a hundred times already!) and the dog decided to make a buffet of the garbage all over the kitchen, your dad might have an expression on his face that would say a lot—without saying a word. A slamming door, a thrown book, a wave, a smile, a whistle—these are all messages!

Let's say that Amy is interested in getting to know Jamal. She might walk up to him and say, "Hello, Jamal, how's it going?" She might simply smile at him and hope he gets the message. Or Jamal might find a little scented note in his locker with an invitation to a party for everyone at her house on the weekend. All of these are ways of communicating her message: I'm interested in you! It could be spoken words, written words, or no words at all.

You are giving messages to other people all the time. And if you look . . . you will see that people are communicating messages to you as well!

What is communication?

1. Communication involves _____ and _____ messages.

2. These messages might be about what you _____, your _____ about something, or how you _____ about something.

3. People can communicate with each other by _____ on their faces.

4. People's behavior can also give _____ to other people.

5. Communication can be through _____ words, written words, or even _____ words at all.

Name_____ Date _____

Communication through Behavior

What message is being communicated by the following behaviors?

1. Laurie raises her hand in class whenever the math teacher asks who knows how to solve a problem.

2. Tom is yawning and stretching at a basketball game.

3. Karla is late coming home from the library because she found some books on painting and lost track of time paging through them. She checked them out and headed straight for her bedroom to spend more time looking at them.

4. Jeff keeps pushing the cat away whenever it tries to sit on his lap.

5. Darla fills up her plate for the fourth time at the all-you-can-eat buffet with her friends.

6. Whatever kind of clothes Susan buys, her younger sister buys also.

7. Tim tried fixing a broken part on his motorcycle for a few hours, then threw his wrench on the garage floor and began to swear.

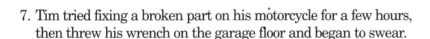

8. Benjamin always invites Tony to go snowmobiling with him and his family on winter weekends.

Communication through Expressions

Match the possible message that is communicated through the expressions drawn below. Write your answer on the line next to each expression.

a. I don't like your smoking in my face.

b. I'm really angry that I got a D on my research paper.

c. This movie is so sad—I can't bear it!

d. Algebra is just beyond me. I'm so confused.

e. If I pretend I don't see him, maybe he'll go away.

f. I'm a friendly person—come on and talk to me!

Name_____ Date _____

Messages

What is the heart of the message that each person below is communicating?

1. Look at all these trophies I got from gymnastics! I was the top gymnast on the team last year. I've got a floor routine that's fabulous. Excuse me while I shine them again.

2. I can't stand people who cheat. Hey, what did you get for number 4? Tell me all of the steps; I don't have time to do it. Do you have the history worksheet done? Can you make me a copy?

3. The next time I see a person wearing a real fur coat, I'm going to tackle them and ask how they would feel if someone shot them and pulled their skin off!

4. It doesn't matter who wins or loses—you have to do your best out there. But if you don't win, don't bother coming home tonight!

5. I'm sorry. I'm returning this paper to you. You made a lot of mistakes on it that I know you can fix. I want you to get a better grade—please redo this.

6. I'm not really interested in drinking. I've got other things to do with my time . . . and my life. Don't bother asking me again.

Name_____ Date _____

Practice Your Communication Skills

Get a partner (or two). Select a situation below (or create your own) and work out a role-play to practice communicating. What is your message to communicate? How will you communicate it?

Situations:

1. You get a low grade on a research paper from your science teacher. You think you followed all of the instructions and you know you put a lot of time into the project. You don't understand why you got this grade and certainly don't think you deserve it. What will you tell your teacher?

2. Your best friend invites you to go canoeing over the weekend. At the last minute, the friend calls and cancels—telling you vaguely that "something came up." You found out that the friend did go canoeing—but with other friends. What will you say to your friend?

3. Your parents invite the daughter of a new neighbor over and insist that you take her out with your group of friends to a party you've been planning to go to. You aren't thrilled with the idea, especially after you see her! You don't think she's going to add to your image as a popular, trend-setting person! What will you do?

4. You hear that someone has been telling everybody that you were drunk last weekend and threw up in your friend's car. This is totally untrue but your friend won't stick up for you and deny it because he might get in trouble for taking his dad's car without permission. Your parents hear about this and want to know what's going on. How will you handle this?

5. Some older kids have been teasing your little brother—stopping him on the streets, chasing him, and really trying to scare him. You have decided to "discuss" this with these kids to get them to stop and leave him alone. What's your approach?

6. Aunt Sadie gives you the ugliest sweater in the universe for your birthday. She wants to know how you like it and hopes that you'll wear it on Sunday. She'll look for you at Sunday dinner! What will we see you wearing on Sunday?

Name_____ Date _____

Appropriate vs. Inappropriate Communication

Decide whether or not the message or the way the message is communicated is appropriate or not for each situation given below.

1. You are scheduled to work at a restaurant this Saturday and Sunday, but want to get off because a friend is visiting you from another state. You decide to call in sick on those days because you figure the boss wouldn't understand and he probably won't find out anyway.

appropriate   **inappropriate**

2. You (a girl) go out with a guy you thought was really nice, but once you get away from the group he has his hands all over you. You really don't want him moving so fast, so you start screaming "Rape" and tell him your father works for the police department and will be looking for him.

appropriate   **inappropriate**

3. You're playing cards with some friends for money and you suspect one of them of cheating. Some of the other players have noticed too and are getting angry. You suggest they cool down, give everybody's money back, and start over just playing for fun.

appropriate   **inappropriate**

4. Your grandmother baked you a homemade cherry pie—even though you thought by now she would realize you don't like any kind of pie. You give her a little kiss on the cheek, take the pie, and share it with everybody who comes over.

appropriate   **inappropriate**

5. Friends of your parents include you in a family outing to a professional basketball game—something you're really excited about! After the game you write them a note, thanking them for inviting you to go with them and telling them what a great time you had.

appropriate   **inappropriate**

Skill 4 —Negotiating or Compromising

INSTRUCTOR PAGE

Rationale: Rarely in life do we get 100% of what we want. Especially in our dealings with others, we have to be able to give and take. This is a definite indication of maturity. Being able to negotiate with others is a way to keep relationships going well without "selling yourself out" or making the other person feel defenseless.

WORKSHEETS

Worksheet #19: Negotiation as a Social Skill

Students are to read the paragraphs explaining what negotiation and compromise consist of, and an example of how a child uses these techniques.

Answer Key:

1. problem; 2. compromise; 3. each

Worksheet #20: Why You Can't Always Have Your Own Way

Examples are given of situations in which individuals think they have more power or rights than they do. Students are to discuss why negotiation or compromise probably won't work.

Answer Key:

1. the person is applying for a job with a bad attitude; there are many other applicants

2. the girl is unrealistically restrictive on the boy

3. the boy wants a car that is too expensive

4. time limits will not allow the boy to delay cleaning up his room

5. sometimes policy can't be changed

Worksheet #21: Situations to Negotiate

Students can practice acting out these situations, discuss possibilities, or write their ideas on the worksheet.

Answer Key: (answers may vary)

1. borrow the money, pay it back with interest

2. agree to keep the pet out in the garage where she won't have to see it

3. trade the sweater, but ask for some money in addition

4. borrow the truck, but do some landscaping for him

5. tell your grandmother that you will get a college degree if she helps you out financially, but you can't promise you'll be a dentist

6. agree that you won't dress exotically around their friends if they don't hassle you about how you dress around your friends

7. ask if you could do the written report this time, if you promise you will give an oral report the next time

8. talk with the coach about your situation and determine whether or not the rules can be bent for you

Worksheet #22: Things That Aren't Negotiable

There are some situations that should not be compromised—those involving moral standards, harmful or illegal situations, and anything that an individual feels strongly about. Students are to discuss the examples and try to come up with others.

Worksheet #23: Practice Negotiating

Students can select partners or form small groups to act out negotiating in the situations on the worksheet.

TEACHER TIPS

- As you set and explain your classroom rules, discuss why some are not negotiable (e.g., for the safety of others), and why in some situations they can be changed.

- Give the students choices in which they can exert their ability to compromise. For example, when setting a test date, have students bring up pros and cons as to what day (Friday? Monday?) would be better.

- Use techniques such as brainstorming to get ideas going. Since most things are not simply black or white, getting ideas going can be a way to get students thinking more openly.

PARENT POINTERS

- As children get older, they need to be given and handle more responsibility—including more decision-making and choices. As situations arise, include your child to the extent possible in making the decisions.

- Help your child through the negotiation process by asking questions rather than leading them to your conclusion. "What might happen if you do this?" "Can you think of another way to achieve that?"

- As you observe negotiating going on (such as parents with their jobs, school situations), try to point out and identify specific techniques that people are using. As with the example of the child, some of it comes naturally—but it is somewhat predictable. Help your child become aware of this.

PRACTICE ACTIVITIES

. . . Look through a newspaper, especially the national news, to examine situations in which negotiating plays a role. It seems that almost every day there are hijackings, kidnappings, ransoms, extortion, labor-management problems, and certainly political issues which are reported. Collect and discuss some of these issues.

. . . Have students select an innocent target—perhaps a parent or sibling—and work on the skill of negotiating for fun and practice. Have the student write down ahead of time what he or she would like to resolve with this person and how it will be achieved.

. . . Have a lawyer visit your classroom to discuss specifics of negotiating between two sides. You may want to bring up the issue of plea bargaining as a technique.

. . . Select a television show (or get a video) that has examples of individuals negotiating for things with each other. As you watch the show as a class, take notes on your observations and compare results.

Worksheet #19   # Negotiation as a Social Skill

Negotiation is a real art! It involves working things out with another person (or group) so that you each get something you want, although neither side may get everything they want. Compromising is similar; this is a way that each side gives in a little bit so that both sides can have something they want. A good negotiator may not even have to compromise; but usually both sides end up giving in a little.

Little kids have this skill down pat! Watch one in action sometime. Little Susie wants to go to the zoo; Mom says she's too busy to take her. Little Susie tries her first tactic— insisting. "But I WANT to go to the zoo!" Mom holds firm: "No, I'm too busy."

Now it gets interesting. Little Susie insists even harder; the stakes are up now! "But I HAVE to go to the zoo! You HAVE to take me to the zoo!" Mom's patience is wearing thin. Her position doesn't budge. "NO, Susie. I already told you, today is not a good day to go to the zoo."

What will Susie do? Her little mind thinks, "Well, I could push even harder—try the old temper tantrum, complete with feet kicking on the floor and face turning blue . . . but that didn't work well last time. I got the famous Time Out." Susie continues to think. An idea pops into her head!

"Mom," she starts out sweetly, "I love you, mommy." She completes the performance with a hug around Mommy's waist. "You're the prettiest mommy in the whole kindergarten."

Now it's Mommy's turn. Mommy sees through this whole act. She has to decide: (a) "Well, you're such a sweet little girl, I'll forget the housework and take you to the zoo," or perhaps (b) "Nice try, Susie, but you're still not going to the zoo today," or even (c) "I love you, too. Today's not a good day to go to the zoo, but why don't we plan to go on Saturday? We can spend the whole day and Daddy will be able to go with us. Maybe you can even bring a friend. So why don't you find something else to do today and we'll save the zoo for a really special trip this weekend."

How does Susie react? "OK, Mommy," and off she goes to play with her dolls.

This little drama shows even a small child can use the process of negotiation to get what she wants. Did she end up getting her way? Well, she didn't get to go to the zoo that day, but she probably will go on Saturday. What kind of compromise was made? Susie agrees to wait and do something else; Mom agrees to delay the trip and go on the weekend.

Win-win!!

What is negotiation, compromising, and how do they work?

1. Negotiating is working out a _____ or situation so that both sides are satisfied with the result.

2. People can make a _____ as a way to negotiate a problem.

3. In a compromise, _____ side gives up something to the other side, but in the end both are in agreement.

Name_____ Date _____

Worksheet #20 **Why You Can't Always Have Your Own Way**

Read these comments by people who are not interested in negotiating or compromising. Why do you think they probably won't get everything they want?

1.

Here's my application for the job. But I want my own office, a company car, and a raise every six months.

Sure, Pal. Put it over there in the stack with the others. We'll call you; don't call us.

2.

We're going steady, Jorge; that means you are not allowed to talk to, look at, or be within five feet of any other female unless it is your sister, mother, or cousin.

You're really nice, Michelle, but I still have friends who happen to be girls!

3.

Dad, I really want this car. It's the only thing I'll ever ask for again! Please!

I agreed to get you a car, but . . . do you really need one that costs as much as our house?

4.

Mom, I promise I'll clean my room tomorrow if you let me go to the party tonight.

Our company is coming tonight. In about 30 minutes. Tomorrow is too late.

5.

I know it says that these tickets are not refundable and that you have to use them only on this date, but it would be better for me if I could go a month from now instead of next week.

Sorry. Company policy. Next?

Name_____ Date _____

Situations to Negotiate

Here are some situations that have "room to compromise." How could you get something you want in return for giving something up or doing something for someone else?

1. You've got a date this weekend, but are low on money. You decide to try to borrow some money from your brother.

2. You want to get an exotic pet, like a snake or a very cool-looking reptile, but your mother isn't sure she wants something like that around.

3. Your best friend offers to trade you a pair of her new jeans for a sweater that you got for your birthday. Your sweater cost a lot more than the jeans, but you don't really like the sweater.

4. You ask your neighbor if you can borrow his pickup truck to haul some trees for landscaping your yard. Your neighbor has offered to let you borrow it before, but has never taken any gas money from you.

5. You want to go to college, but you don't have the money, so you might end up working for a year or two. Then you find out that you have a rich grandmother who always wanted a dentist in the family.

6. You want to get your nose pierced, but your parents both object to this. They also objected to your dyeing your hair purple and getting a tattoo. They are so unreasonable! What can you do?

7. The teacher requires an oral report as a requirement for biology class. You get so nervous when you have to speak in front of a group and wonder if you could do something else instead.

8. The track coach says that practice is going to be seven days a week—including Sunday. You and your family always go to church on Sunday and, besides, you work a part-time job in the afternoon. It seems that time is going to be a problem.

Things That Aren't Negotiable

You may find yourself in situations in which you don't want to compromise and should not compromise. Can you think of some examples for the following situations?

Don't Compromise on Your Standards

I'm sorry. I'm staying a virgin until I'm married. It's not negotiable.

I'm not going to do a really sloppy job on your car—my name goes on my work. You're going to get my best effort.

Don't Compromise on Things That Are Illegal or Harmful

I suppose I could cheat on my taxes—maybe I won't get caught... But I'm not sure it's worth that chance.

Don't tell me that everyone is smoking pot. I'm an example of the exception. Everyone does NOT smoke pot.

You're asking me to testify that I saw the accident and that it was not your fault. You're my friend, but I know that's a lie.

Don't Compromise on Things You Think Are Wrong

In my religion, we believe it is wrong to drink alcohol. Please don't ask me to join you.

I know you're my supervisor, but I saw you changing the prices on those clothes. I'm not going to do that.

Name_____ Date _____

Practice Negotiating

Here are some hypothetical (but possible) situations to consider. Read them over and decide what you could, should, and would do.

1. You are the president of the ski club. Half of the group wants to spend a lot of money and go to a really nice resort during spring break. The other half wants to go to two or three local resorts on three separate weekends, which would cost a lot less money. What could you do?

2. There is a gang at your school that takes money from other kids in return for NOT beating them up. You know that there are other students who resent this, but no one will seem to speak up or take a stand against them.

3. The end-of-the-year dance has always been open to anyone from the class who wanted to go, whether he or she had a date or not. Now there is a group who wants only couples to attend the dance. They also think it should be formal and that everyone should arrive in a limousine. You disagree.

4. Your father expects you to take over the family business—running a funeral home. You are much more interested in going into computers and being involved in a business. Dad won't support your efforts to do anything other than train for the family business.

5. You and your brother have to share one car while you are both in high school. Since you both have jobs, go to school, and have a fairly active social life, this can sometimes be a problem. Friday night is an example—you want to take some friends to a movie, he wants to go out on a date with a new girlfriend.

6. Your parents agree to let you have a dog, but it can't be too big, too loud, or too much trouble. You have your heart set on a St. Bernard puppy—huge, loud, and not housebroken.

7. You're at a party and everyone seems to be drinking. You find yourself surrounded by your "friends" who tell you that if you take one drink, they'll leave you alone.

8. You and sister both want the same dress that happens to be on sale at your favorite store this weekend. Obviously, you both can't wear the same dress at the same time or place, but you both really want it!

Skill 5 —Assessing a Situation

INSTRUCTOR PAGE

Rationale: Being able to "size up a situation" is a social skill that enables one to say or do appropriate things in reaction to that situation. By knowing what's going on, the student can make conclusions as to what to do. It is the "clueless" person who makes embarrassing comments, asks inappropriate questions, and overreacts to situations. This is a very important skill to be aware of!

WORKSHEETS

Worksheet #24: What's Going on Here?

Students are to read the information about assessing situations and complete the summary statements at the end.

Answer Key:

1. going; 2. practice, clues; 3. setting; 4. mood, down/sad, cheerful/happy; 5. knowledge;

6. social

Worksheet #25: Assessing the Same Situation Differently

This worksheet depicts a comic look at how "typical" males and females may view the same situation. You may want to bring up the topic of stereotypes!

Answer Key: (answers may vary)

1. students may conclude that the women didn't really understand the game and were not that interested in it; the men knew every statistic about the game and the play

2. the guy knew that someone got married, but that was about it; the girl could describe who was at the wedding, what they were wearing, and the ingredients in the food

Worksheet #26: What's Your Call?

Students are to pick the best answer that describes what is probably happening in the situations on the worksheet.

Answer Key:

1. (b) clues—birthday, other light on

2. (c) conversation stopped; staring began

3. (a) it's pretty obvious that Bob is using notes on the test

4. (b) they're avoiding each other

5. (a) he's shy; he appears to be uncomfortable

Worksheet #27: How Tense Would This Situation Make Someone?

Using a Tense-o-Meter, students are to indicate how tense, or stressful, the given situation would probably make someone feel. They can personalize this by thinking of how they would feel, then think more generally—how would most individuals assess this situation?

Worksheet #28: Timing and Moods

Some times are not good times to interrupt, to ask questions, or to offer unwanted advice. Assessing situations accurately can help students determine whether or not this is one of those times.

Answer Key:

1. a. no; b. no; c. yes; 2. a. maybe; b. yes; c. yes; 3. a. no; b. no; c. yes; 4. a. no; b. yes; c. yes;

5. a. yes; b. yes; c. no; 6. a. no; b. no; c. yes

Worksheet #29: An Appropriate Reaction

Students are given a situation to assess, and then they are to determine (by drawing or writing) an appropriate reaction.

Answer Key: (answers will vary)

1. the employee should do everything possible to make sure all rules and regulations are followed carefully

2. the girls may want to spend some time with Jenny, take her out to eat, etc.

3. students should make plans for when to go to the library that day

4. the girl might talk with Bob about what he did after school—perhaps his appointment was cancelled, or . . . ?

TEACHER TIPS

- As situations arise, point out clues and patterns. For example, Mondays at school may be slow, Fridays may be restless, days when there is a game may be more relaxed, etc.

- Let students know how YOU feel and how situations affect you personally. Without giving too much unwanted information, let students know if you had a rough night with a cranky baby or if you had car trouble that morning. This affects their situation at school as well!

- When school policies are an issue, talk about how they affect the individual students. Examples might be athletes being tested for drugs. How will that affect each and every student?

PARENT POINTERS

- Talk about what types of things/situations affect people. Christmas shopping can be stressful, hot weather can make some people crabby, a wonderful spring day with sunshine might tend to make everyone in the community seem nicer, etc.

- As you watch or listen to the news, talk with your child about the events and how they affect the emotional climate of your city, state, or the nation. If there is a war going on that involves sending troops, including the boy next door, how might that affect how you feel about it?

- As they arise, discuss family events with your child and how they will affect every member. Moving, job changes, financial reversals, paying off debts, getting a bonus, or winning a contest can all affect other members of the family. Practice assessing the situation!

PRACTICE ACTIVITIES

. . . Have students draw or find pictures to represent various situations and their analysis of them. This could include the setting itself (a haunted house, a peaceful sea, a dentist's office), and the emotions they invoke (fear, laughter, puzzlement, curiosity). Some students may want to write stories about the pictures including events leading up to the moment in the picture.

. . . Have students describe situations in which they were completely inaccurate in their impressions. Did you completely misunderstand a situation and were later embarrassed? Did someone pull off a tremendous surprise for you?

. . . What is a "typical day"? Students may select such a day and describe the settings, situations, moods experienced, and finally arrive at some conclusions.

Name_____ Date _____

What's Going on Here?

Assessing a situation means being able to tell (quickly, if possible—and accurately!!!) what's going on in a given situation. If you hear someone screaming, it might mean a person is in danger and needs help immediately. On the other hand, perhaps that person just won $1,000,000 and is really, really happy about it. Knowing the difference can mean determining whether to call 911 or make a new friend quickly!

Assessing situations takes practice. You have to look for clues as to what's going on. For example, if you're walking down a dark alley when you hear the screaming, you might tend to think a situation is dangerous. If you're at a party and hear screaming, you'd probably tend to think people are just having fun. The setting, or where something happens, is a clue.

Another clue is determining the mood of the situation. The mood at a funeral home will probably be very different from that of a graduation party. Being aware of how people probably will be feeling is another clue to assessing a situation.

Yet another clue is what you know about a situation. If you see two dogs going at each other's throats and growling, you might just laugh and say, "Those are my dogs, Tessa and Foxy. They are always playing like that." You can say that because you know the dogs. You have knowledge about them and what they are likely to do. On the other hand, if you see two strangers punching and shoving each other, calling each other names that your mother wouldn't let you say, and— yikes!—even some blood—well, you might want to make plans to leave. You don't have enough clues to determine whether or not this is a safe situation for you.

Being quick to size up what's going on is not only a good social skill, it can also be a good safety skill.

What does it mean to assess a situation?

1. Assessing a situation means to be able to tell what's _____ on in that situation.

2. Assessing a situation takes _____. It helps if you look for _____.

3. One clue is the _____ , or the place where the situation is.

4. Another clue is the _____ of the people or situation. A sad occasion would make people tend to feel _____ ; a happy occasion would probably make people feel _____ .

5. Another clue is your own _____ of the situation. If you're familiar with the people and places involved, you'll be better able to know if something is normal or not.

6. Being able to assess a situation is not only a good _____ skill, it can also help your safety.

Worksheet #25 **Assessing the Same Situation Differently**

What conclusions do these groups of people draw from looking at the same situation? Why? Do you agree with these cartoons?

Situation: Watching Football

Female . . .

Male . . .

Situation: Going to a Wedding

Male . . .

Female . . .

Name_____ Date _____

What's Your Call?

Some situations are described below. Select your best guess of what's happening in the situation. Look for clues.

1. You just turned 16. Your house is dark, although your parents are supposed to be home. You are a little nervous about going into the house. What's going on?

   (a) Your parents have been abducted by aliens.

   (b) Everyone is waiting to surprise you on your birthday.

   (c) The power went out in your house, although there is a light in your brother's bathroom.

2. You walk into a room and suddenly everyone stops talking and turns to stare at you. What's going on?

   (a) You forgot to put clothes on.

   (b) Everyone is practicing being a mime.

   (c) They were probably talking about you.

3. The teacher passes out your semester exam. Bob, who has been copying answers from you all year, is secretly pulling out little pieces of paper from under his sleeve and then writing something on the test. What's going on?

   (a) Bob is cheating—using written answers to help him on the test.

   (b) Bob forgot to pick the lint off his shirt that morning.

   (c) Bob doesn't think you are smart enough to copy from anymore.

4. Two girls show up at a party wearing the same sweater. They avoid each other all evening. What's going on?

   (a) They are really twins, separated at birth.

   (b) They are embarrassed that they have the same sweater on.

   (c) The girls are mad at each other about something else.

5. John, who is a little shy, is being teased by some other kids about wearing a t-shirt that has the name of a losing baseball team on it. He appears to be uncomfortable. What's going on?

   (a) He's uncomfortable about the teasing.

   (b) He likes the teasing, because it makes him feel included.

   (c) He should have been more careful about what teams he supports.

Name_____ Date _____

How Tense Would This Situation Make Someone?

Being aware of how tense a situation would probably make someone feel can help you assess what's going on. Think about the following situations and decide how tense you would feel (on a scale of 1-10, with 10 the most tense).

TENSE-O-METER

_____ 1. You are taking a quiz on material you know very well.

_____ 2. You are taking a final exam on your toughest subject.

_____ 3. You are taking the SAT, hoping to get scores good enough to get into the college of your choice.

_____ 4. You are in a doctor's office to find out if you (or your girlfriend) is pregnant.

_____ 5. You are in a doctor's office to find out if you have poison ivy.

_____ 6. You are in a doctor's office to find out if your sister is HIV positive.

_____ 7. You are driving on an icy road.

_____ 8. You are driving with five loud passengers, each of whom wants a different radio station.

_____ 9. You are getting ready to go out on a blind date with your cousin's friend.

_____ 10. You are getting ready for a first date with the person you've been admiring all semester.

_____ 11. You're getting your hair styled by someone from the Beauty Academy.

_____ 12. You come home to find your parents yelling at each other.

_____ 13. You oversleep and wake up to find out that you're an hour late for work.

_____ 14. You walk into a room of ten people—all boys (if you're a girl); all girls (if you're a boy).

_____ 15. You have to stand up in class and give a 3-minute spontaneous talk about how you feel about political events in Haiti.

Name_____ Date _____

Timing and Moods

You may have heard the expression: "Timing is everything." Consider each situation and decide whether or not it is a good time to ask for or do something.

1.

Here's your test. You have 20 minutes.

Is this a good time to:

a. ask to go to the bathroom?

b. ask if the test counts?

c. forget about everything else on your mind except the test?

2. Your brother is jailed for possession of drugs. Again.

Is this a good time to:

a. borrow your brother's shoes?

b. ask your parents if you can do anything to help?

c. give up smoking?

3. Your best friend is in love.

Is this a good time to:

a. tell him/her you saw the other one with another guy/girl?

b. talk about your break-up with your boy- or girlfriend?

c. listen to your friend talk?

4. Your father has lost his job.

Is this a good time to:

a. tell your dad there's an opening at Dairy Barn?

b. start looking for a part-time job to start paying your own bills?

c. tell your dad how much you appreciate him?

5. Your co-worker got a promotion and you didn't.

Is this a good time to:

a. congratulate him/her?

b. start working harder to get noticed too?

c. talk about how unfair it is?

6. Your boss finds out that someone has been stealing money from the cash box.

Is this a good time to:

a. insist that you didn't do it?

b. offer to fingerprint everyone?

c. wait for instructions from your boss?

An Appropriate Reaction

Now that you are good at sizing up a situation, you should be able to come up with an appropriate response or reaction to the following situations. What would you do or say in each?

1.

NOTICE: The health department is coming to do an inspection today. Be aware employees.

2.

Did you hear about Jenny? Her mom has cancer and is going to the hospital for a bone marrow transplant.

3.

Classes are shortened today because of an assembly, so you might not have time to get to the library before it closes at 3. Plan ahead so that you get the books you need before the weekend. Thank you.

4.

Hmmm . . . Bob, my dear boyfriend, told me he had a dentist's appointment after school. But that looks like him with Amy . . .

Skill 6 —"Reading" Other People

INSTRUCTOR PAGE

Rationale: Related to being able to size up a situation is the ability to size up other people. This involves understanding what message a person is giving—whether it is spoken or implied by facial expressions, tone of voice, body language, and the sincerity of the message itself. Individuals who lack this skill are usually not aware of how others react to them or what kind of impression they are giving.

WORKSHEETS

Worksheet #30: A New Kind of Reading

Students are to read the information on ways to learn about other people and complete the sentences at the bottom.

Answer Key:

1. cover, looks; 2. clues; 3. clues, facial, tone, body; 4. what; 5. cover, person

Worksheet #31: Facial Expressions

Students match a picture depicting a facial expression with the emotion it shows.

Answer Key:

1. e (color in cheeks, tight eyebrows)
2. c (blank expression, wide-eyed, wavy mouth)
3. d (eyes cast aside, expressionless)
4. f (wide-eyed, shaking, furrowed brow)
5. a (smile, eyebrows lifted)
6. b (wide-eyed, mouth opened)

Worksheet #32: Tone of Voice

Two pictures could convey two different meanings for the same actual words; however, the message is different. Students are to match the message with the two possible situations.

Answer Key:

1. b, g; 2. c, e; 3. a, h; 4. d, f

Worksheet #33: Body Language

Students are to match the unspoken messages with the message conveyed by the way the person is acting or using his or her body.

Answer Key:

1. b; 2. d; 3. g; 4. e; 5. c; 6. a; 7. h; 8. f

Worksheet #34: Sincerity

Students are to evaluate the spoken comments in situations on the worksheet and to rate the sincerity of the speaker. Then they are to decide what the speaker's probable purpose was in making the comments.

Answer Key:

1. no; to make fun of someone
2. yes; to give advice, be helpful
3. yes; to be polite

4. possibly—we don't know if he can really surf or not; to be included in the group

5. no; to encourage the boy

6. yes; to express appreciation

Worksheet #35: Teasing

Students are to decide whether or not the teasing in each situation is positive (not harmful or mean) or negative (intended to hurt someone).

Answer Key:

1. + she doesn't really mind him coming back

2. − she is making fun of Kara's accident

3. + he is teasing himself

4. − he is making fun of Mitch

5. + she is just kidding; being sympathetic

6. + he is teasing the teacher

Worksheet #36: Read Me!

Situations are given for students to act out in skits for others. The audience should try to pick out the clues the actors give to indicate how the characters feel.

TEACHER TIPS

- Create a unit on emotions—identifying them, describing them, causes, etc. Provide opportunities for students to voluntarily share their examples of some emotional experiences.

- Videotape a popular television episode. Turn off the sound and observe the characters. Discuss what clues are given to help you pick up on the conversations. Then replay the tape with the sound.

- Display pictures from magazines of famous people. How has the media decided to "read" these people? Is the public opinion deserved (e.g., Dennis Rodman—haughty? President Clinton—outgoing, friendly)? Are these characterizations deserved?

- Have students read a spy novel or a biography of a spy. Discuss how it is beneficial to be able to read other people as well as to be unreadable in front of others.

PARENT POINTERS

- Your child may be very adept at hiding his or her emotions. Or, your child may be overly expressive and overreact to everything. At neutral moments when both you and your child are calm, talk about emotions and how differently people express themselves.

- Pay attention to the tone of your voice when you are making requests/giving orders. How does your child interpret what you say and how you say it? Ask for feedback!

- Ask your child to share his or her yearbook with you (perhaps from the previous year). Ask for descriptions of some of the people in the book. Can you tell "just by looking" that a person is outgoing, funny, etc.? Does a moment of a captured expression reveal what his or her personality is like? Ask your child.

- Models, actors, dancers, and other performers have to be able to portray an emotion they may not truly feel at the time. Expose your child to these performances if possible (school play? local talent contest?). Talk about when it is a real asset to be able to "pretend."

PRACTICE ACTIVITIES

. . . Have students keep a "mood" journal for two weeks. What puts them in a certain mood? Can they control how they feel?

. . . Spend some time observing people in a public place such as a restaurant or local mall. What do you note of the expressions and body language of people? Have students record their observations.

. . . Have a friend take photographs (or go to one of those instant photo booths) of a student's expressions. Pick several: sadness, anger, boredom, etc. Have them analyze their facial characteristics. What does boredom "look like" on them?

. . . Make videotapes (humorous is OK) depicting how body language (exaggerated!) can convey various messages to others.

. . . Rent an old silent movie. Note how much expression and communication is conveyed without the use of words. Write your observations.

Name_____ Date _____

A New Kind of Reading

You probably are able to read books. Maybe when you go to the library to do that book report, you look for a book with an interesting cover. Maybe you look at how many pages are in the book. Perhaps you look to see who is the author, hoping that this book will be as good as his or her last one! Then you might open it to check out if there are lots of pictures inside or if it is filled with tiny writing. All of these are clues as to what the book might be about.

Did you know that you can also learn to "read" people? Just like assessing or sizing up a situation by looking for and thinking about clues, you can also look for clues from other people to make good guesses as to what they are all about. What are they thinking? Are they friendly? Are they interested in you? Are you interested in getting to know them?

Some of the clues you can use to read people are: looking at their facial expression (scowling? smiling?), listening to their tone of voice (loud? timid?), body language (clenched fists? arms crossed?), and what people say, as well as how they say it.

You may have heard the expression: "Don't judge a book by its cover." That means don't assume just because it doesn't have an exciting cover, it's not worth reading. It's the same with people. Don't assume that because someone seems shy or boring, she's not secretly taking sky diving or tuning up her Harley-Davidson on weekends. Expand your "reading"!

What does it mean to "read" other people?

1. When you select a book to read, you might look at the _____ to see what it's about. In the same way, you might size up the way a person _____ to get an impression of what he or she is like.

2. People give _____ as to what they are like.

3. Some of the _____ you can use to read people are looking at their _____ expressions, listening to the _____ of their voice, or paying attention to the way they hold their _____ — body language.

4. You should notice _____ people say as well as how they say something.

5. Don't judge a book by its _____ ; and don't judge a _____ by the way he or she looks.

Name_____ Date _____

Facial Expressions

A person's face can show you how he or she feels at the moment. Match the emotion with the face that shows that emotion. What do you think each person is thinking about or what may have happened?

_____ 1. angry

_____ 2. confused

_____ 3. bored

_____ 4. stressed or tense

_____ 5. pleasant

_____ 6. surprised

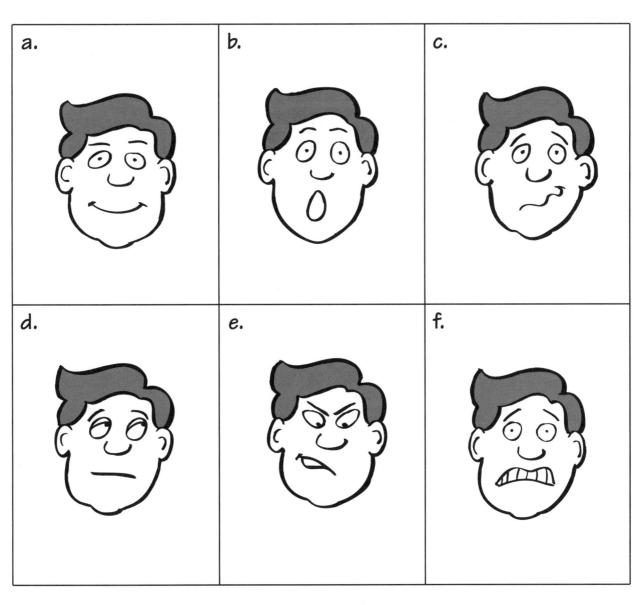

a.

b.

c.

d.

e.

f.

Tone of Voice

The way your voice says your words can change the entire meaning of the words. Each phrase below could have two meanings, depending on how the tone of the voice says the words. Match each phrase with the two possible situations.

_____, _____ 1. "Well, I did a great job on that!"

_____, _____ 2. "Hurry, or you'll be late for dinner."

_____, _____ 3. "I'll be glad when this is over."

_____, _____ 4. "Stop!"

Name_____ Date _____

Body Language

You can get clues as to what people are like or what their "message" is by what they do with their body. Match the message with the body below.

_____ 1. "You are standing too close to me—give me some space."

_____ 2. "I disagree with what you are saying."

_____ 3. "Tell me more; I'm interested."

_____ 4. "I'm really neat. I love the attention!"

_____ 5. "I'm not interested in what you're saying. I'll find something better going on somewhere else."

_____ 6. "I don't like to be touched."

_____ 7. "I like to be touched."

_____ 8. "I'm very boring and no one is probably interested in me."

Sincerity

How sincere—or honest—are the following comments? Complete the chart by evaluating the speaker and the situation and decide if the speaker is sincere (yes/no/don't know). Then make a guess as to the speaker's intentions—what does he or she want or what is the purpose for the comments?

Comment	Sincere??	Purpose
1. You look great in those glasses!		
2. I think you look better in red than pink.		
3. Thank you for the meal.		
4. I just love to surf! I surf all the time!!		
5. You did a really nice job on mowing the lawn.		
6. I really appreciate your help!		

Name_____ Date _____

Teasing

Teasing is a special case of tone of voice in which the message is intentionally not the same as what the words alone would seem to say. For example, someone who says "I'm so dumb" may really be saying, "I made a silly mistake," or "Come on, correct what I just said! Tell me I'm not!" Decide whether each instance of teasing shown below is positive or negative in its purpose. Explain why.

Read Me!

Act out the following situations with a partner or other players. Give clues for your audience and look for clues if you are the audience.

Clues:

facial expression, tone of voice, body language, sincerity/teasing

Situation #1

You work at an office. Your boss is very worried about her son who is sick. You are trying to make the boss feel more comfortable.

Situation #2

You are on a first date with someone you don't know very well. He/she seems more interested in everything else around than you.

Situation #3

You have a good-looking young student teacher in your science class. He/she seems to want the students to think that he/she is very "cool" and "one of them."

Situation #4

Your mother's mystery novel that she has been working on for six years has just been accepted by a publisher.

Situation #5

You just rear-ended someone in your brother's car and you're afraid your brother might be angry at you.

Situation #6

The teacher hands you a quiz about the bones of the body and your mind goes completely blank.

Skill 7—Making a Good Impression

INSTRUCTOR PAGE

Rationale: Making a good impression on others is the flip side of "reading other people." The tables are turned; now WE are the ones who are giving a message or creating an image that others will see and judge. The image you convey to other people may or may not be a "true" picture of you—but nevertheless, people often judge others very quickly.

WORKSHEETS

Worksheet #37: What Is a Good Impression?

After reading the paragraphs comparing job applicants, students are to complete sentences that summarize the impressions made.

Answer Key:

1. look; 2. habit; 3. friendly, confident, experience; 4. impression

Worksheet #38: Your Appearance

Students are to select which of the two characters for each situation appears to be more suited for the situation.

Answer Key:

1. first; 2. second; 3. first; 4. first; 5. second; 6. first; 7. first; 8. second

Worksheet #39: Your Attitude

On this worksheet, characters are giving impressions to others about their attitude. Students are to match the attitude given with the impression that it makes.

Answer Key:

1. f ; 2. d; 3. a; 4. c; 5. e; 6. b

Worksheet #40: Getting Prepared

Students are to think about the situations on the worksheet and come up with ideas for how they could best prepare to give a good impression for the message you want to convey.

Worksheet #41: Asking Appropriate Questions

Students are to discuss the inappropriateness of the questions asked by the characters on the worksheet.

Answer Key: (answers may vary)

1. bad taste
2. embarrassing for the person
3. too personal
4. implies you made a mistake
5. nosey, not his business
6. obnoxious

TEACHER TIPS

- Invite a personnel manager of a business to talk to the class about hiring of employees. What kind of applicants do they look for? What factors create a favorable impression? Have students write a few questions ahead of time that they want to ask this person.
- Arrange for your class to take a field trip to a fairly nice restaurant—perhaps in connection

with a trip to a museum or other local educational attraction. Stress that they are to dress nicely (be specific), demonstrate good manners, and work on what they need to practice for creating a good impression on the people they come in contact with. Ask for feedback from these people on the impression your class has made.

- Invite another class in your school to visit your class for some sort of project display, play or skits, or other type of presentation for the purpose of preparing to create a good impression. Talk with students about preparing the room (signs, posters, programs, decorations), the activities (well-organized, program) and the way they will interact with the guests (making introductions, thanking them for coming).

PARENT POINTERS

- Share with your child some experiences you may have had interviewing for a job, volunteer work, or other situation in which you wanted to create a good impression. Your child may not be aware of the jobs you have held in the past or some of your experiences.

- Always remember to introduce your child to your friends or acquaintances. This gives them a quick opportunity to create a good impression on someone.

- Ask your child for advice on what he or she thinks you should wear to a specific outing or an occasion, or what you should take along with you in preparation.

- Show your approval of your child's appearance by sincerely complementing him or her whenever possible.

PRACTICE ACTIVITIES

. . . Have students role-play the situations on Worksheet #40. You may want to videotape these skits and analyze what made or did not make a good impression.

. . . Have students write a semi-humorous handbook (complete with pictures) of Do's and Don'ts for various social situations in which they would want to make a specific impression. Ideas could include: What to Wear on a Date to a Hockey Game, 50 Starter Statements for Meeting That Special Someone, How to Impress Your Science Teacher, etc.

. . . Through interviewing or just chatting with parents and grandparents, have students come up with illustrations of what used to create a good impression 30 or 50 years ago and how different some of these situations are today. Some examples may include the areas of fashion (boys wore suits and ties to a lot more places, girls wore hats and gloves), conversation (ladies did not talk about certain subjects in mixed groups), and habits (smoking, drinking, etc.).

Name_____ Date _____

What Is a Good Impression?

You are the owner of a jewelry store and need some extra help at the counter. After placing an ad in the paper, you have received several phone calls. You are planning to interview several possible workers. "Hello," a young man says to you. "I'm here to apply for the job." You notice his ripped jeans and his old shirt. His hair is long and messed up. You wonder how long it has been since he washed it! Or took a bath! "Sorry," you hear yourself saying. "I don't think you're right for the job." You had an idea of the kind of person you wanted to hire—someone who looked quite different from the young man who showed up. You were disappointed. He didn't appear to be someone you wanted for the position. You didn't like the way he looked.

Another applicant comes by. At first you are quite interested in the pretty, blonde girl who comes to your office. Her hair is combed nicely, her clothes are expensive, and—thank goodness—you are sure you smell the newest perfume. "Well, so you are here to apply for the job of a clerk," you say to her. "What's your name?" She opens her mouth and does not stop talking for 20 minutes. She has told you her life story, every detail from kindergarten to shopping at the mall yesterday. You are certain that any customer who asked her a question would get much more than they bargained for. You don't like this habit.

Next.

Your next applicant is an older woman. "Good afternoon," she greets you. Her smile is friendly and she appears to be very self-confident. You find out she has had lots of experience in sales. She also compliments you on your ruby ring. Now you know she knows something about jewelry! "Are you able to work on weekends?" you ask her. "No problem," she answers. "I'm available whenever you need me." You close the file. "You are hired," you tell her. "I have seen all I need to see." This applicant may be a thief. She may even be a liar. But she made a good impression on you!

What is meant by making a "good impression"?

1. The first applicant for the job didn't _____ right.

2. The second applicant looked nice, but she had a very annoying _____ .

3. The third applicant appeared to be _____ and very self _____ . She also had lots of _____ in sales.

4. This applicant made a good _____ because she seemed to be what the employer wanted to see.

Name_____ Date _____

Your Appearance

Choose which of the two characters below has the better appearance for each situation.

1. going trick-or-treating

2. playing football in the mud

3. going swimming

4. going to a formal party

5. riding a horse

6. taking your dog for a walk in the woods

7. going for a job interview for mowing lawns

8. going for a job interview for working at a hamburger place

Your Attitude

Match the attitude demonstrated below by the characters with the impression that it gives.

_____ **1.** I don't want to talk.

_____ **2.** I know what I'm doing.

_____ **3.** I want you to respect me.

_____ **4.** I'm interested in you.

_____ **5.** I'm eager to learn.

_____ **6.** I'm very patient.

a.

b.

c.

d.

e.

f.

Name_____ Date _____

Getting Prepared

   If you know you need to make a good impression, get yourself ready! What would you need to do to make your best impression in these cases?

   1. talking to the parents of a child you hope to babysit

   2. meeting a cute boy/girl after a game

   3. trying out for the school play

   4. volunteering as a nurse's aide at the hospital

   5. picking up your family's foreign exchange student at the airport

   6. interviewing for a job at the city zoo as an animal caretaker

   7. tutoring elementary students after school

   8. explaining to the track coach why you missed practice

   9. meeting the grandparents of your best friend

   10. trying to get votes to be elected class president

Name_____ Date _____

Worksheet #41 # Asking Appropriate Questions

What is wrong with asking these questions in the situations below?

_____

1.

I heard your dad was sick. Do you think he's going to die?

_____

2.

Hey, your skin looks a whole lot better since you've been going to the skin doctor. Are you still going for treatments?

_____

3.

Did you dye your hair?

_____

4.

Are you really going to wear those shoes in public?

_____

5.

Was that your mother I saw at the welfare department yesterday? Doesn't she have a job yet?

_____

6.

Where are you going? When will you be back? Is Johnny going with you? May I go too?

_____

Skill 8—Controlling Your Emotions

INSTRUCTOR PAGE

Rationale: Although we may sometimes feel extremely angry, disappointed, hurt, or another emotion, it is not always in our best interest to show that emotion. It may trigger anger in another person, may hurt someone's feelings, may end up embarrassing ourselves or others, and a host of other events. Sometimes by controlling the first, or natural reaction, we can come up with a better, more socially acceptable, response.

WORKSHEETS

Worksheet #42: Why Should We Control Our Emotions?

Students are to read a short story about Mark, who experiences anger in two different situations, but shows his feelings differently in each.

Answer Key: (answers may vary)

1. angry, "Quit it!", yelled at his sister

2. angry, probably nothing, watch the Home Shopping Network

Worksheet #43: First Reaction

Students are to offer their ideas as to what their first reaction or emotion would be in each situation on the worksheet.

Answer Key: (answers may vary)

1. angry; 2. annoyed; 3. startled; 4. disgusted; 5. fear; 6. impatience; 7. impatience; 8. anger;

9. embarrassment; 10. startled; 11. anger; 12. laughter

Worksheet #44: What Triggers Your Emotions?

Sometimes certain situations (a bully, a sad movie, a close friend, etc.) will trigger the same emotion. By knowing that a certain situation will make you feel a certain way, you may have some control over choosing to be in a situation that will make you feel an emotion strongly.

Worksheet #45: Controlling What You Show

What you feel and what you show may be two very different things. On this worksheet, students are to discuss what each character feels and then what he or she actually shows or displays to others.

Worksheet #46: Alternative Reactions

There are alternatives to how we express what we truly feel. Students are to think of different possibilities to show the emotion felt in the examples given.

TEACHER TIPS

- Use yourself as an example when possible. If you are in a bad mood, had something bad happen, are distracted by something good, etc., cue your students in. Show that even though your feelings go one way, you are controlling what you do—carry on anyway, do your job, continue to be polite, etc.

- Through your subject areas, invite students to speculate about what emotions are triggered or felt by someone else. Historical biographies, stories in English class, and even story problems in math can be a starting point.

- Be sure to notice and praise students when they are appropriately reacting to situations. It's sometimes hard not to laugh, swear, tease, or punch someone out!

- Rent and/or show a popular video in class that will lend itself to a lot of discussion. Perhaps something semi-controversial (check with your principal!), but yet appropriate, would stimulate some strong emotions. Caution students to think before they speak!

- Stop class discussions occasionally to ask: "What are you thinking now?" Give students a chance to reflect on their feelings.

PARENT POINTERS

- Pay attention to the faces you make while on the phone—which may not mirror what you are saying. For example, you may be pretending to be listening, but actually watching TV. At the right time, signal your child to pay attention to what you are doing.

- Think of creative ways to handle telephone solicitors. You may not be interested in giving money to every cause that comes your way, but enlist your child's help in coming up with a decent, but firm, response.

- Explain to your child exactly what you are feeling, and then continue to explain how you are going to respond to that feeling. For example, "I'm really angry that you weren't where you were supposed to be; it made me late for work when I had to pick you up. However, I'm going to put my anger aside for right now because I need to concentrate on that presentation at work."

- Anger is an emotion that can be very harmful. Talk about ways you and your child can appropriately express anger (do something physical, talk about it later, count to 10—or 100, etc.).

PRACTICE ACTIVITIES

. . . Have students make masks (perhaps in conjunction with an art project?) for themselves. Talk about how a mask "hides" oneself from others. What masks do we create for ourselves that show what we want to show/hide to others?

. . . Select a personal goal for each student that will help him or her focus on controlling a specific emotion, behavior, or habit. Talk about ways that this will be attempted.

. . . Assign students the project of attending a basketball or football game (or other sport). Have them observe the emotions expressed (joy, excitement, disappointment, etc.).

Why Should We Control Our Emotions?

Mark was watching his favorite mystery show on TV. The victim was identified and the murderer was just about to be revealed, when suddenly his older sister came home, picked up the remote, changed the channel (and did she even ASK? No!), and put on The Home Shopping Network.

1. How do you think Mark felt? _____

_____

What do you think Mark said? _____

What do you think Mark did? _____

Mark probably felt very free to express how he felt to his sister. He and his sister have a long, open relationship and neither one feels that they are going to hurt the other's feelings by saying EXACTLY what they feel.

Now let's put Mark in a doctor's waiting room with a lot of other people. Put in a lady with a screaming baby. Add a few ten-year-old boys who are tossing around a beanbag and trying to swat it down with a magazine off the waiting room table. Throw in an old man (with extremely bad breath) who is mumbling to himself. All Mark came in for was a health physical so he could play football! But at least Mystery Theater is on in the background. Mark settles down to watch his favorite show until he is called.

Did I say Mystery Theater was on? Only for a second. The lady with the screaming baby decides to change the channel to her favorite soap opera. Mark is not thrilled. In fact, after being hit in the head with a beanbag, he is in a slightly crabbier mood than before.

"Hey, change the channel!" command the ten-year-olds. "We don't want to watch that stupid show!" Mark finds that he is in agreement with the beanbag throwers. The lady agrees. But what channel does she end up with? Home Shopping!!!!

2. How do you think Mark feels? _____

What, if anything, do you think Mark will say? _____

What will Mark do? _____

In both situations, Mark was unhappy that his television watching was interrupted. In the first situation, he probably felt perfectly comfortable telling his sister exactly how he felt. But in the second situation, he was surrounded by strangers. Perhaps he was expected to behave differently. Perhaps he thought about embarrassing himself by complaining or becoming angry. We don't really know Mark well, but we could probably assume he would not act the same way in the second situation. In that one, he needed to control his emotions. Even though his first reaction would be one of anger or annoyance, Mark would use his social skill training to take a different course. Why?

_____

_____

First Reaction

What would be your first reaction to the following situations?

1. The boy who sits behind you in History copied your paper—and turned it in as his paper!

   _____

2. At a basketball game, you are sitting next to two very loud, obnoxious fans of the opposite team.

   _____

3. A friend starts out his/her conversation with you with: "Would you want to know if I heard someone gossiping about you?"

   _____

4. Your Math teacher says you aren't working up to your potential—at all!

   _____

5. You get a pass to go to the counselor's office, IMMEDIATELY!

   _____

6. The elderly person driving in front of you forgets(?) to signal and cuts you off.

   _____

7. The young driver in front of you signals forever before finally turning into your lane.

   _____

8. The teenage driver in front of you gives you an obscene gesture and yells something about the poor condition of your car.

   _____

9. Your grandmother introduces you to her friend as her "little pumpkin."

   _____

10. Your friend signals you that your zipper is down—and that cute girl you wanted to meet is coming down the hallway towards you.

    _____

11. Someone whom you thought was a friend laughs hysterically at your new haircut.

    _____

12. A substitute teacher walks into class, sits down behind the desk, and falls over—chair and all.

    _____

Worksheet #44   # What Triggers Your Emotions?

Think about the things that you KNOW will set you off, make you laugh, make you cry, or trigger other emotions.

I know it's only a cartoon—but does Bambi's mother always have to die?

1. What makes you ANGRY?

    _____

    _____

2. What makes you SAD?

    _____

    _____

3. What makes you feel SILLY?

    _____

    _____

4. What makes you CRY?

    _____

    _____

5. What makes you feel HAPPY?

    _____

    _____

6. What makes you EMBARRASSED?

    _____

    _____

7. What makes you PROUD?

    _____

    _____

8. What makes you feel DEPRESSED?

    _____

    _____

Name_____ Date _____

Controlling What You Show

The following characters have some very strong feelings about what happened to them. But what they showed is different from what they felt. Try to identify both emotions in each case. Why is the second one more "socially acceptable"?

What Happened	**What He/She Feels**	**What He/She Shows**

1. Arnold didn't make the football team, even though he practiced all summer, every day.

2. Sharon got a birthday gift: a perfectly horrid pin from great-aunt Stella.

3. Steve's boss was in a BAD mood. Nothing Steve did was right. Finally the boss yelled at him and told him to do the dishes over.

4. Maggie got an A+ on a difficult test in English. Her best friend (also her study-buddy), got a D.

5. Nathan moved to a new school district where he is one of a few minority students.

Name_____ Date _____

Worksheet #46

Alternative Reactions

Maybe you can't change what you feel, but you can learn to control what you show, say, or how you react. Use some of these ideas or think of alternative reactions to these emotions.

- give it time—sometimes that is enough to change things
- use humor
- talk to someone
- explain your feelings
- change your plans

ANGER
Jeff lent his bike to someone, who broke it.

tell how you feel

go out for ice cream anyway

DISAPPOINTMENT
No one remembered Sally's birthday.

SADNESS
Kae's parents are probably going to get a divorce.

call an understanding friend

make a joke about it

EMBARRASSMENT
Angie fell down the steps and her books flew everywhere!

apologize

REGRET
Todd told his sister that all of his friends thought she was fat—then realized he had hurt her feelings.

Skill 9—Revealing Yourself to Others

INSTRUCTOR PAGE

Rationale: We all carry secrets around with us—or know of things about ourselves that we may or may not choose to share with others. Perhaps we have a bad memory of the past, regret a mistake, are embarrassed about something. . . For whatever reason, we are selective about what we let others know about ourselves. However, selectively revealing things about ourselves can build bridges to others.

WORKSHEETS

Worksheet #47: Mysterious or Just Plain Quiet?

Students are to read the short story about a girl who does not reveal much about herself and the various reactions from others to her.

Worksheet #48: Why Tell About Yourself?

Students are to match the reasons why it is a good social skill to reveal things about yourself with the example. Students may need some clues to make the correct matches.

Answer Key:

1. b; Alison is telling that she was new last semester and making a point to be polite to another person
2. d; she is making conversation about vacations
3. e; they both have dogs in common (and probably housebreaking)
4. c; the boy is opening up about being worried about a test
5. a; the boy is carrying a tennis racquet
6. f; the girl is revealing a problem she had with her sister

Worksheet #49: Revealing Things to Be Polite

This worksheet has situations in which students are to think of ways that an individual can be polite to someone else. They don't necessarily have to initiate a conversation or deep friendship, but just a surface level of politeness or courtesy.

Answer Key: (answers may vary)

1. tell about some things you are doing in school (sports, activities)
2. ask a question that leads to something you are interested in
3. ask her how she likes the weather
4. you could talk about how you like the dentist
5. you could mention how busy you are at school with all of your activities

Worksheet #50: Revealing Things to Make Conversation

Students are to think of things to say to another person that would continue a conversation. This is a deeper level than simple politeness.

Answer Key: (answers may vary)

1. What did you do today, Dad?
2. Where did you get them pierced? Did it hurt?
3. Oh, are you interested in bowling?
4. That's a neat dog you have!
5. Have a seat! Have you heard anything about this movie?
6. Do you know of any other games that are fun?

Worksheet #51: Finding a Common Point with Others

Students are to draw a picture or write a short story that illustrates how two people can find something in common. They are to try to use the comments on the worksheet.

Worksheet #52: Making a Selective Impression

After looking at the characters on the worksheet, students are to decide what impression the people are trying to make on others.

Answer Key:

1. he is a fan of the Green Bay Packers (sweatshirt)
2. she is concerned about her weight and looks
3. she is a good student (books)
4. she is rich (fur coat, earrings, expensive car)
5. he is very friendly (talks to everyone)

Worksheet #53: Take a Risk, Open Up

The characters on the worksheet are all revealing something about themselves that might be considered a little "risky" or personal. Students are to discuss how revealing this information might help them become better friends with someone.

TEACHER TIPS

- Some students like to talk about themselves and may reveal too much about themselves, their families, or their situations. Talk about what is appropriate for general conversation. Emphasize that students should know their audience and be able to trust people to whom they are talking.

- If a student is going through a rough time that you are aware of or has experienced a tragedy, caution other students to think before they talk or do something—even with the best of intentions. You may want to use this opportunity to reveal something about yourself that will help you connect with the student.

- When you come across something particularly interesting about a student, let him or her know that you find this fascinating and encourage the student to share this with others. A shy student may have an interesting hobby or collection—use this information if possible !

PARENT POINTERS

- Since you know your child better than most of his or her teachers probably do, encourage your child to share interesting things about him- or herself with others at school. Students may do a report, for example, on a state that you have visited or lived in. In some ways, the child can be an "authority" on some topic.

- Find out what topics are coming up in school and help your child see what connections he or she can make from personal experiences.

- If you run across a child (friend of the family?) who is going through a problem or difficult situation, alert your child to the situation (with discretion) and see if he or she might be interested in helping out in an appropriate way.

PRACTICE ACTIVITIES

. . . As an ice-breaker activity, make up a sheet listing interesting attributes about students and then have them circulate around the room to obtain signatures that match. For example, you may have a grid containing comments such as: "Has been to Alaska"; "Has 5 dogs"; or "Has eyes that are two different colors." Be sure there is at least one comment to match each student and that the comments are non-threatening.

. . . Pair students into partners and give them 60 seconds to find out something about each other that is (a) interesting, (b) funny, (c) unique, or (d) a favorite memory. Have the students speak for each other when they reveal what they found out about each other to the group.

. . . If a student reveals something to the class that is quite personal, discuss the secrecy of it with the class as well as the content. For example, you may say something like: "Paulina really took a risk sharing what happened to her back in Montana when she was shot. This is not something you would tell everybody. Be sure to use good judgment, class, with this information. It cost her something to share that with us."

. . . Invite a motivation guest speaker who has dealt with a problem or been through an unusual situation to talk to your class. You may get someone who will answer any question thrown at him or her (a good sport!). Prepare students ahead of time as to the background of the speaker and try to head off inappropriate comments or questions.

Worksheet #47   # Mysterious or Just Plain Quiet?

"Come and join us, Katie," Debbie invited. The tall dark-haired girl looked at her feet and then, almost reluctantly, joined the group of kids at the lunch table. "Would you like to try some of this stuff my mother made?" Debbie continued. Katie shook her head and appeared to be concentrating on her sandwich as though it was going to move by itself.

"Did you get your report for social studies done?" asked Todd. When it was obvious that Katie wasn't going to answer, he redirected his question to the entire group. "Well, am I the only one who didn't make the deadline?" Everyone laughed. Everyone, that is, except for Katie. No one was quite sure what emotion she was expressing—except for great interest in her potato chips.

Later, Katie was the topic of discussion. "I think she's stuck up" was Alisha's conclusion. "She doesn't talk to anyone, ever! She acts like she doesn't like us, even when we go out of our way to include her. She acts like she's better than we are."

"No, I don't think so," said Bryan. "I think she's just bored. Who can blame her in this town!" He laughed.

"Well, I think she's really shy," said Debbie. "And I'm going to keep on inviting her to join us. I know she doesn't say anything, but she always comes . . ."

"Why bother?" asked April. "I think she's got mental problems. She never looks anyone in the eye."

"I agree," said Bernard. "I think she's really a secret agent and this is all an act to throw us off. She's probably really a rock star who doesn't want any attention."

Debbie shrugged. "Who knows?" she said. "She's a mystery."

1. What is your first impression of Katie?

2. Do you think Katie wants to be a part of the group?

3. How would you respond to Katie? What, if anything, would you do?

4. Would it bother you that Katie does not want to (or is not able to) reveal anything about herself?

5. What would you want to find out about Katie?

Worksheet #48

Why Tell About Yourself?

Below are some reasons why it is a good social skill to be able to reveal things about yourself. Match the reason with the example on the right.

_____ **1.** It's polite.

a. *I love to play tennis. Want to see my trophies?*

_____ **2.** It helps to make conversation.

b. *I'm Alison. I'm glad to meet you. I was the new kid last semester!*

_____ **3.** You can find a common point with another person.

c. *I'm really worried about that test; I didn't study very much. Did you?*

_____ **4.** If you open up first, the other person might respond by opening up also.

d. *How was your vacation? We went to Mexico last summer. Did you go to Mexico City? Tell me what you did.*

_____ **5.** You can control the impression you give to others.

e. *Have you ever had to housebreak a puppy? What a pain! I know you have dogs, too.*

_____ **6.** It can help you feel better to reveal something to others.

f. *I am so worried about my sister. I found some drugs in her room. It's all I can think about. . .*

Name_____ Date _____

Revealing Things to Be Polite

How could these individuals reveal things about themselves in order to be polite to others?

1. You are at the dinner table with your grandparents and their friends. They are talking about the good old days. It seems as though the only questions they ask you are silly—like what grade are you in, who is your favorite teacher, and how did you get so grown up? What could you reveal about yourself to be polite?

2. You are out on a date with a new friend. All he/she wants to talk about is himself/herself, which is getting to be pretty boring for you! What could you do to be polite?

3. You are in an elevator going up to the 26th floor to meet your father at his office. It's a long ride and you find yourself staring at the woman who is in the elevator with you. Well, somebody has to say something first. What might you say to pass the time?

4. You are in a waiting room at the dentist's office. The old man next to you won't quit interrupting you—and you are in the middle of a great article in a magazine that your parents don't get. He keeps talking about his dentures. What could you reveal about yourself that would be polite?

5. The new neighbors finally moved in, and it looks as though there are going to be some youngsters living next door. You find that your mother has given you a glowing recommendation as a fabulous babysitter—and the neighbor seems very interested. As you walk down the driveway, you see the woman with her children. It's a good opportunity to say something polite. What?

Name_____ Date _____

Revealing Things to Make Conversation

Finding something to talk about may take a little bit of thinking. What are some things you could say, do, or reveal about yourself that would keep each conversation going?

Name_____ Date _____

Finding a Common Point
with Others

Draw or write a short story showing how two people could find a common point with each other using these examples. You may want to include the following bit of conversation in your cartoon or story.

1. "Didn't I see you at the sky-diving school last weekend?"

2. "I can't stand Roberto. He is so mean."
   "Really? I can't stand him either!"

3. "These are beautiful pictures of your horse!"

4. "Did I hear someone say that you used to live in New York City?"

5. "Yes, I am related to Nick, the star of the basketball team. He's my older brother."

6. "You have great taste in jeans. Where did you get those?"

7. "Your name was on the list for making the bowling team. I'm the captain of the team."

Name_____ Date _____

Making a Selective Impression

What impression might be made from the following characters? Pay attention to what they wear, what they say, and what "props" they carry.

Name_____ Date _____

Take a Risk, Open Up

In order to "connect" with someone else, these characters are opening up, or revealing something about themselves that perhaps they wouldn't ordinarily reveal. How could this help them make a friend or be a friend to someone else?

TONY

I heard you were going to Dr. T. for appointments after school. I went to him for about a year when I was going through a rough time with my parents. He really helped me think things through.

MARIE

My mother died of cancer last year. It's still hard to talk about it. There are some days when I still can't believe it's real. But I think I understand how you must feel. . . .

GREGORY

I was kicked off the football team last season because I was late for practice too many times. You don't mess around with Coach!

TIFFANY

Look, don't have sex until you are ready. I did, and now I'm a mother. And I'm sorry to miss out on so much that is going on at school.

Skill 10—Working with Others

INSTRUCTOR PAGE

Rationale: Many tasks involve cooperation from others. Using a teamwork approach can make a hard job easier, complete it more efficiently, and also be a socialization experience. Learning to work well with others, whether as a leader/organizer or one who follows directions, is perhaps the most fundamental social skill.

WORKSHEETS

Worksheet #54: Sharing a Job

After reading the short story about three siblings who are given the job of cleaning out the basement, students are to answer questions based on the story about how the three used a teamwork approach to complete the job.

Answer Key:

1. authority; 2. divide; 3. ideas, brainstorming; 4. responsibility

Worksheet #55: Working as a Team

Students are given sample jobs and are asked to identify possible team members who would help complete the job, and then to decide/discuss how failure of a worker to do his or her part would affect the total job.

Answer Key: (answers may vary)

1. a. contractor, builders, carpet-layers, plumber, electrician, etc.; b. the house would not be well-built, lead to problems later
2. a. pilot, traffic controller; b. CRASH
3. a. doctors, nurses, hospital administrator, pharmacist, etc.; b. surgery may not go well, patient could suffer or die
4. a. actors, stagehands, musicians, etc.; b. many mistakes might be made in a performance
5. a. astronauts, scientists, monitors, etc.; b. the astronauts would not be safe
6. a. hotel manager, bellboy, clerk, concierge, room service personnel, maids, parking attendants, etc.; b. a person may have a bad experience and not come back
7. a. driver, attendants for the car, timer, etc.; b. safety of everyone around may be involved
8. a. workers on the assembly line; b. the car may be unsafe to drive

Worksheet #56: Cooperating with Authority

Students are to identify which characters are demonstrating cooperation when given an assignment or request from an authority figure.

Answer Key:

1. no; 2. yes; 3. yes; 4. no; 5. no

Worksheet #57: Brainstorming

Students are to match the idea presented by the characters brainstorming with the concept.

Answer Key:

1. b; 2. c; 3. d; 4. a

Worksheet #58: Carrying Out Your Responsibilities

Given several tasks, students are to pretend they are the leader assigned to carry it out efficiently. They should list responsibilities they would delegate to others.

TEACHER TIPS

- Use terms such as brainstorming, responsibility, authority, and division of labor with your class as tasks come up.

- Teach and use brainstorming whenever possible from simple tasks ("How many jobs can you think of that start with A"?) to more complex problems ("What are some things our community could do about littering?"). Start with generating all kinds of possibilities, even outrageous ones, then narrow your solutions to more realistic, workable ones.

- Invite your class to provide input into ways to divide up chores—both pleasant and unpleasant. How does the concept of fairness come into play?

PARENT POINTERS

- Occasionally, hold family meetings in which family chores are divided up (daily, weekly, etc.). Decide how the family members will work as a team, how they will complete the tasks, who will monitor/supervise whom, and what evaluation techniques will be used.

- Set aside regular times for the entire family to tackle a big, needed job such as cleaning the house, cleaning up the yard, taking care of repairs, raking the leaves, etc. You may find that working together can actually be fun!

- Plan a pleasant (even, FUN) job for the family to work on. Perhaps build something for the family (a picnic table? plant a vegetable garden?), prepare for a party (family reunion—hosted at your house?), or make a seasonal activity more organized (putting up/taking down the Christmas tree, cleaning out closets in the spring, getting out the summer lawn furniture, etc.).

PRACTICE ACTIVITIES

. . . Assign cooperative tasks with clearly defined outcomes. Create roles/responsibilities and have students take turns experiencing each role. For example, they may rotate being the leader/organizer of a task, recording the events or procedures, handling quality control, and simply being a good worker. While some students may fit certain roles much better (some are natural leaders, while others prefer to follow), it is good for each to experience what it is like to have a somewhat different role.

. . . Have students look through the local newspaper to find examples of authority in the lives of people—government, local leaders, police, etc. Discuss how the general public views these authority figures and (by the examples found) how they react to them. Letters to the editor may be a good source as well.

. . . Put on a class performance or presentation in which everyone has some role to carry out. Put students in charge of thinking through the job and deciding what role/responsibility goes with the task. Is it best suited by being a leader? By just doing what they have been assigned? By thinking and revising?

. . . Have students select a specific task that might be representative of a career they are interested in (taking a flight to Europe, selling advertising, running a restaurant, having surgery, teaching preschoolers, etc.). Then have each one make a poster that depicts how many other individuals are involved in carrying out that task. The task could be in the center with offshoots representing supporting personnel.

Name_____ Date _____

Sharing a Job

"Guess what? Dad wants us to clean out the basement," Emily informed her sister and brother.

"Oh, no," groaned Michael. "I wanted to go roller blading—do we have to do it now?"

"Yes," Emily informed him. "He wants it done by noon or none of us can go out tonight."

"Well, looks like we have no choice," said Lynette. "Let's do it. What first?"

The kids thought for a minute. "Why don't we divide up the chores?" suggested Lynette. "I could sort through the toys, Mike could sweep, and Emily could straighten up the boxes."

Mike sat down. "Well, I have an idea. Why don't you let me straighten up the boxes, since they're heavy. And they're mostly my stuff anyway."

"What about this?" said Emily. "How about if we all sweep first—that will finish that job quickly. Then we can all separate our own boxes. It would go faster …?"

They agreed. The three got their old clothes on and got to work. In no time, the basement was sparkling clean.

"Great job!" said Dad after a thorough inspection. "Now it's clean enough for us to have a party down here."

"Great idea!" yelled the kids. "We can mess it all up again!"

Use the following words to complete the sentences below:

brainstorming	ideas	divide	responsibility	authority

1. The kids worked as a team to complete the entire job. First, they agree to accept the job assigned to them. They accepted their father's _____ .

2. Next, they decided to _____ the tasks so everyone had a different job. Each one picked something he or she could do well.

3. Mike brought up some other _____ to consider. One idea led to another and pretty soon the others had ideas. This is an example of _____ .

4. Finally, they completed the jobs they had chosen to do. They took _____ for their work.

Name_____ Date _____

Working as a Team

Many tasks are complex and require more than one person to complete. Think about the following jobs and (a) identify team members who are a part of this job and (b) decide how it would affect the entire job if someone didn't do his or her part.

Job	Team Workers	Consequences for Not Taking Responsibility
1. building a new home		
2. flying an airplane		
3. doing brain surgery		
4. putting on a play		
5. taking a space voyage to the moon		
6. running a hotel		
7. racing a car at the Indy 500		
8. assembling a new car		

Name_____ Date _____

Cooperating with Authority

Which characters below are cooperating with the following authority figures?

1.

I want these research papers turned in no later than Friday at 3:30.

I have plans. I'll just turn it in sometime next week—it doesn't matter.

Teacher

2.

I'd like to see your driver's license and registration.

Here they are, Officer.

Police Officer

3.

Pass on the next play. They won't be expecting that at all.

COACH

That doesn't seem right—but we'll do it.

Coach

4.

I have you scheduled to work on the next three week-ends. We're going to be busy and I'll need you to supervise all these new employees.

I'll be calling in sick!

Boss

5.

You must give up smoking, start exercising daily, and quit eating so much garbage!!

You're crazy! I'm not giving up chocolate!

Doctor

Worksheet #57

Brainstorming

Brainstorming is a technique in which people can work together to come up with ideas. Match the brainstormers on the left with what's happening to their ideas on the right.

Task: Putting on a Play

_____ 1.

a. discarding poor choices

b. generating all kinds of ideas

_____ 2.

c. bringing out useful knowledge

_____ 3.

d. refining an idea to make it better

_____ 4.

Worksheet #58 **Carrying Out Your Responsibilities**

You are the leader for the following tasks and must assign others to help you complete the job. What are the responsibilities you assign to everyone on your team?

Task #1: Planning a ski trip for 20 students

_____

_____

_____

Task #2: Painting a huge mural on the side of a brick wall

_____

_____

_____

Task #3: Preparing a meal for 10 people for a birthday surprise

_____

_____

_____

Task #4: Cleaning out the garage for elderly neighbors

_____

_____

_____

Task #5: Building a doghouse

_____

_____

_____

Skill 11—Making Others Feel Comfortable

INSTRUCTOR PAGE

Rationale: You may encounter situations in which people are caught in embarrassing situations, are misunderstood, under pressure, or simply in trouble. Going out of your way to try to make the individual feel comfortable (without being overbearing or nosey) is one way to be "a good neighbor."

WORKSHEETS

Worksheet #59: The Play

This worksheet contains a short story about a girl who makes a mistake about which day to wear her pirate costume to school. Her friend, luckily, saves her some embarrassment by offering to lend her some clothes.

Answer Key: (answers may vary)

1. embarrassed
2. laughed with her (not at her), offered to lend her clothes, moral support for talking with the teacher
3. ask the teacher to let her call her mother; ask around for extra clothes

Worksheet #60: Embarrassing Moments for Others

Students are to discuss or draw a picture to show how suggested techniques might help someone out of an embarrassing situation.

Answer Key: (answers may vary)

a. give help; b. use humor; c. give help; d. be sympathetic; e. use humor; f. stick up for him or her

Worksheet #61: Helping Others Through Stressful or Uncomfortable Situations

Students are to read and discuss the situations to come up with ideas for how to help someone out.

Answer Key: (answers may vary)

1. use humor; 2. talk to the coach privately; 3. stick up for your friend; 4. give support—you can do it!; 5. talk to the teacher; 6. pick Jon

Worksheet #62: Ordinary Times to Be Outgoing

Sometimes simple conversation can make a situation more pleasant. Students are to role-play the situations on the worksheet, emphasizing how a few words can make someone feel more comfortable.

Answer Key: (answers may vary)

1. "Have you seen the view from the top?"
2. "Welcome! Need a tour?"
3. "Your son is really a star! What a great player!"
4. "Excuse me, you left something here!"
5. "What a cute dog! He'll catch on!"
6. "Hi. Welcome back!"
7. "Congratulations! Good job!"
8. "Need a hand?"

Worksheet #63: Things to Beware Of!

You have to be careful not to be too helpful, too talkative, or overbearing. Students are to discuss the situations on the worksheet and tell why the talkative person is not being helpful.

1. potentially embarrassing situation for the boy—he doesn't want to talk about why he's in the office
2. it's nice to help someone out, but don't advertise it!
3. the boy just wants to figure it out by himself
4. maybe the girl doesn't feel bad about being pregnant
5. not his business
6. maybe the girl isn't rich; not polite to ask the price of shoes

TEACHER TIPS

- Set a good example by diffusing embarrassing moments for your students by using humor, being practical, or being comforting.
- Take a moment to tell about an embarrassing moment of your own and how you handled it. One thing will lead to another, and soon your students may be sharing embarrassing stories.
- Compliment students who take initiative to include others in social settings.
- Try to avoid situations in which groups are formed by "popularity polls." Form cooperative groups randomly or by other objective means.
- If a student in your class encounters a tragedy (death in family, illness, etc.), have the class plan ways to support this person (cards, letters, visits, etc.).

PARENT POINTERS

- Help your child think through situations in which he or she may find himself or herself in a jam. ("Are you SURE you want to wear that today? Why don't you take along a sweatshirt . . . ")
- Model good social skills by demonstrating how to help others be more comfortable. Maybe your child should overhear you comforting someone on the phone, being understanding to an overworked sales clerk who may have made a mistake on a bad day, or just being friendly to someone in a waiting room. This is a practical lesson in everyday living.
- Ask your child what he or she thinks about the kids who don't fit in. Is it a matter of clothes? looks? attitude? What opinion does your child have about this? Is there anything he or she could do that would help the misfit? Would he or she even want to?

PRACTICE ACTIVITIES

. . . Have students collect examples of embarrassing moments from teen magazines or other appropriate sources. After laughing about them, talk about how it was handled. Will it matter in 100 years?

. . . Give the students an open-ended situation and have them finish the story. For example, detail a story in which a child with a terminal disease has moved into your neighborhood. It is not contagious, but it will certainly affect the life of your neighbors. One day you are asked if you will babysit for the child on a regular basis. What happens . . . ?

. . . Television commercials can be mini-social lessons. Have students analyze the interactions portrayed in selected commercials. How do the characters make comfortable contact with each other in seconds (borrowing coffee, working for a cause, walking the dog, etc.)?

Name_____ Date _____

The Play

Jamie's class was putting on a play, and Jamie had a rather large part with a lot of lines. She also got to wear a neat costume with a pirate patch over her eye, a huge golden hoop earring, and a brightly-colored shirt.

"How do I look?" she asked her mom as she adjusted the eye patch. "Do I look like a swashbuckling pirate? We have dress rehearsal this morning before school, and I want to be all ready!" She whirled the cardboard dagger around as she jumped across the room.

"You look lovely, dear," said her mother, sipping on her coffee. "Are you ready to go? I can drop you off at school on my way to work."

"Ready, peasant!" Jamie yelled. "Let's go before I make you walk the plank!"

Jamie's mom dropped her off in front of the school and Jamie headed for her classroom.

"I must be a little early," she thought, noticing that no one else was in the room. She dropped her books off on her desk and walked around the room. Finally, she took off her eye patch and put the sword down on the floor. "Where is everybody?"

The morning bell rang and students began filling the hallway. Her classmates began entering the room—none of them in costume.

"Hey, that's a pretty good costume," noticed Amelia. "But why did you dress up today? Our performance isn't until Friday."

"Friday?" gasped Jamie. "Today is . . ."

"Thursday," laughed Amelia. "Did you bring anything else to wear?"

"NO!! I've got to get to a phone!" Jamie cried. "I've got to reach my mom as soon as she gets to the office! I wonder if this beard will come off . . . " She started rubbing on her darkened cheeks and chin without success. "It's going to be a long day!"

"Don't worry," laughed Amelia. "I have some extra clothes that I brought for after track practice. I bet we can get that beard off, too. Let's ask Mrs. Lasky if we can go to the restroom."

1. How does Jamie feel?

2. How did Amelia help her feel comfortable in an uncomfortable situation?

3. Without Amelia's help, what could Jamie have done?

Name_____ Date _____

Embarrassing Moments
for Others

How could you use these techniques to help others feel comfortable during an embarrassing moment? Draw a picture or explain your ideas.

use humor	**stick up for him or her**
give help	**be sympathetic**

a. Abdul was walking down the steps at school when he tripped, dropped his books, and fell flat on his back in front of everyone!

b. A strange boy comes up to you, puts his arm around you, and says: "Hi, Sweetie. What's up? What??? Oh, you're not Jenny! I thought you were Jenny!!"

c. A girl in your class has a huge rip in the back of her pants that she doesn't notice . . . yet.

d. Your math teacher is reading the class's grades out loud. Donald, a boy you don't know very well, got an F. It is the lowest grade in the class. You notice Donald shrinking down in his seat.

e. Your friend is supposed to introduce you to a good-looking friend, but suddenly forgets your name.

f. The basketball coach says to your friend: "Aren't you the kid who threw the ball in the wrong basket at the game last night?"

Worksheet #61

Helping Others Through
Stressful or Uncomfortable Situations

How could you smooth out these situations in which someone is stressed out or feels uncomfortable?

1. This order is all wrong—the drinks are mixed up, the dinners aren't cooked—this is not right at all!

My first day on the job!

2. The uniforms cost $25. The money is due on Friday.

My parents can't afford that . . .

3. I'm inviting all of the girls in the class to my party—except Jeanine.

Doesn't she know Jeanine is right here?

4. Everyone has to sing a solo. Sing into the tape recorder and we'll play it back so everyone can hear.

Sean is so shy! This will be hard for him!

5. Today we're going to talk about AIDS.

I wander if he knows that Alan's brother has AIDS?

6. OK, two teams!! Who wants to be captains? Start picking who you want on your team!!

No one will pick Jon. They never do!

I hate this!

Name_____ Date _____

Ordinary Times to Be Outgoing

Role-play the following situations. How could you help make each one a comfortable situation?

1. You are riding to the 50th floor in an office building. There is one other person on the elevator. It's going to be a looooong ride!

2. You're in the office when you notice a new student enrolling. She seems frightened and unhappy. You find out she's from France and doesn't speak English very well.

3. You're at a football game. Everyone in your section is cheering for your team. The man sitting next to you is the father of one of the star players. He is very excited about the game.

4. You're checking out at the food store. You notice that the elderly woman in front of you left a birthday card at the register.

5. You're at the dog training class with Rover. Another person is there with a very unusual looking dog—that is very ill-behaved!

6. Everyone at school knows that Mike was suspended for bringing a knife to school last semester— and now he's back in school. He acts as though he doesn't have a friend in the world.

7. A popular girl, whom you don't know very well, won an award for swimming. You've never talked to her before, but you're going to pass her in the hallway in about ten seconds.

8. You see a little girl having trouble working the pay phone on a busy street in front of a store. She looks as though she's about cry.

Things to Beware Of!

You have to be careful not to try too hard when trying to make someone comfortable—your help may not be wanted or needed. What's the problem in the following situations?

1.

*What are you in here for? They said I cheated, but I didn't! I'm **always** getting picked on. It's so unfair. Last year, I . . .*

OFFIC

Be quiet!

2.

I'll be Joan's partner because I know that no one else will want to work with her. But I will. I'm just that kind of person!!

*I don't **want** to be her partner!*

3.

Do you want me to help you with that? I know the answer!!!

No, I can figure it out.

4.

Don't feel bad about being pregnant! Why, you can hardly even tell.

Now everyone will know!

5.

I notice you're taking the same medicine that my brother takes. I know it really helped him with his depression. He was practically going to jump out of a window one time!

Mind your own business!!

6.

Those are neat shoes. You must really be rich to afford shoes like that. They're really nice. Where did you get them? How much were they?

Nosey!!

Skill 12—Making and Keeping Friends

INSTRUCTOR PAGE

Rationale: Having friends is one of the nicest consequences of developing good social skills. Friends not only add a lot of satisfaction to our lives but they also can benefit from what you have to offer.

WORKSHEETS

Worksheet #64: My Good Friend?

After reading the comic about a jealous girl and her definition of what a friend is, students are to answer the questions about friendship.

Answer Key: (answers may vary)

1. Renee thinks a friend should be at her beck and call, overreacted to Shantelle's action, blames without investigating, etc.

2. Shantelle is jealous, possessive, and doesn't listen.

3. We don't know why Renee didn't wait for Shantelle (perhaps she had a reason), but something happened to change her plans; still, she wanted Renee's company for another activity so she must not be too estranged from her.

Worksheet #65: Is This a Good Friend? (Part I)

Students are to read the descriptions of friends and circle their responses to indicate if they agree or not. The heart of this worksheet is in the discussion that should follow. What definition or descriptions can students come up with that define or describe a friend?

Answer Key: (answers may vary)

1. false—who is ever always in a good mood?; 2. true; 3. true; 4. false—things change; 5. true—or at least tries to understand!; 6. answers may vary—what is good advice?; 7. true (but explain)—what is "there for you"?; 8. false—but circumstances may affect this; 9. false—this is a possessive, jealous friendship; 10. hopefully, true most of the time—but who can listen all of the time?; 11. false—you may be wrong; 12. false—you may ask for something that isn't good for you

Worksheet #66: Is This a Good Friend? (Part II)

This is a continuation of the topic of worksheet #65. This gives examples of how a restricted friendship can't really operate well. By comparing your expectations for friendship with reality, you can hopefully understand that friends are people, complete with limitations and needs of their own.

Answer Key: (answers may vary)

1. corresponds to item #1 on worksheet #65; 2. corresponds to item #4; 3. corresponds to item #5; 4. corresponds to item #6; 5. corresponds to item #7; 6. corresponds to item #8; 7. corresponds to item #9; 8. corresponds to item #11; 9. corresponds to item #12

Worksheet #67: Ways to Make Friends

This worksheet gives a few ideas on ways to make friends. Students should read and explain the items, then apply them to their own situations.

Answers will vary.

Worksheet #68: Are You a Good Friend?

Students are to read the situations in which another individual is involved and come up a response. How understanding, forgiving, or possessive of a friend are they?

Answer Key: (answers will vary)

1. introduce Cynthia to several others who will be at the party
2. stop lending things
3. start being busier when she calls
4. meet Mark at neutral places
5. invite her to come to your house
6. start inviting Tony to join you when you go out with other friends

TEACHER TIPS

- When having a class discussion on friendship, have students think of their oldest friend (one that they've had the longest), newest friend, best friend, and closest friend. Discuss how each achieve this status.

- Talk about what friends have in common—sports, other hobbies, interests, leisure activities, etc. Then talk about how some friends may be "opposites" in some ways, yet still be close friends. How can this be?

PARENT POINTERS

- Provide opportunities for your child to bring friends to the house. Know who he or she is hanging around with and what the common attraction is. What do they do with their time together?

- Encourage your child to participate in healthy activities in which he or she may find friends. A church group, YMCA activities, summer camp, and any kind of organized lessons are just a few examples of places where your child will meet others.

- If you take a short trip or family excursion to the movies or museum, ask your child to invite a friend. Include the friend in conversations and other activities.

- When your child's friends do come over, show a sincere interest in him or her, but try not to be overly inquisitive. Remember to respect their privacy, but let them know you are there—and available. Sometimes other people's children find it easier to talk to a friend's parent than their own!

PRACTICE ACTIVITIES

. . . Create a class "holiday" to celebrate Friendship. Design activities for students (and enlist their ideas) simply to pay tribute to good friends. This could include cards, deeds, special events, and maybe a newspaper write-up.

. . . Assign research projects to students to find out who the friends of famous people (past and present) are—and how they influenced the person. (The friendship of Helen Keller and Annie Sullivan is one example!)

. . . Assign journal activities in which students write about various aspects of friendship. Entries might include: What's the best thing your friend ever did for you? (And vice versa) Have you ever felt "betrayed" by a friend? Do you agree with this statement: to have a friend you first must be one?

. . . Challenge students to select a person whom they don't know well and go out of their way to find out more about him or her.

. . . Help students complete a social chart in which they list a best friend in the center circle, close friends in the next circle, and casual friends in the third circle.

Name_____   Date _____

My Good Friend?

1. What do you think Renee's definition of a friend is?

2. How good of a friend would you say Shantelle is to Renee?

3. How good of a friend would you say Renee is to Shantelle?

Is This a Good Friend? (Part I)

Read the following statements. Circle TRUE if you think it is true or FALSE if you disagree with the statement.

1. A friend is always in a good mood.	**True**	**False**
2. A friend doesn't talk about you behind your back.	**True**	**False**
3. A friend sticks up for you.	**True**	**False**
4. A friend is someone who will always be close to you.	**True**	**False**
5. A friend is someone who understands you and how you think.	**True**	**False**
6. A friend is someone who gives good advice.	**True**	**False**
7. A friend is someone who is always there for you.	**True**	**False**
8. A friend is someone who would lie for you.	**True**	**False**
9. A friend doesn't have other friends—only you.	**True**	**False**
10. A friend is someone who will listen to your problems.	**True**	**False**
11. A friend is someone who agrees with you all of the time.	**True**	**False**
12. A friend is someone who would give you whatever you asked.	**True**	**False**

© 1998 by John Wiley & Sons, Inc.

Is This a Good Friend? (Part II)

Look through your responses to worksheet #65. Did you come up with some ideas about what describes a good friend? How are the following examples exceptions to the characteristics described on worksheet #65?

1. I just don't have time to talk to you right now. My dad has been yelling at me for not cleaning my room and I'm really in a bad mood. Talk to you later.

2. Oh, hi there! I haven't seen YOU since you moved away in second grade! How've you been?

3. You know, Fred, I don't understand a thing about your religion, but I know it's important to you . . . Wanna go play football?

4. I think definitely you should quit your job and go to junior college. At least, that's what my parents keep telling me.

5. Sorry I couldn't make your recital. I got stuck with my brother's paper route.

6. I told your parents you were at my house last night so they won't be hassling you about going drinking with everybody. You should be OK!

7. I can't make it to your game tomorrow—I'm going to Sandy's birthday party. I'll have to see you later.

8. It really bothers me that you smoke. There are so many people who are trying to quit—and there isn't one thing good about it! I wish you'd stop.

9. Sure you can borrow my research report. I hope you get an A on it like I did!

Worksheet #67

Ways to Make Friends

Here are some ideas for ways to make new friends. How could they apply to you and your life?

1. Be available.

2. Show your personality.

3. Be willing to change a
   negative first impression of
   someone.

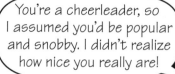

4. Make the first move.

5. Be willing to make an effort
   to find friends.

6. Don't overlook people.

  Too old. Too loud.

  Too young. Too rich.

 Wrong sex. Seems boring.

Name_____ Date _____

Are You a Good Friend?

What would you do in the following situations? What does your response indicate about how you feel about friendship?

1. CYNTHIA is very shy and doesn't like parties. You've been invited to a pool party at another friend's house and you'd really like to go. What can you do about Cynthia?

2. DENNIS is always borrowing your stuff—your CDs, your jean jacket, and even your car, but when you ask him about borrowing his tennis equipment or a video that he just got, he always seems to have an excuse. What can you do about this?

3. AMANDA has her share of problems—divorcing parents, an obnoxious brother, allergies, and constant run-ins with teachers at school. Whenever you call, she wants to go on and on about her problems. At first they seemed important and you didn't mind listening, but now it's like the same story over and over. What can you do?

4. You are really becoming close friends with MARK, a friendly, outgoing guy with a lot of interests—but you can't stand his parents. Whenever you go over to his house they want to know everything about you, your family, your plans—everything! You'd like to hang out with Mark, but that family is something else!!!

5. JANELLE is a terrific artist, and she's willing to give you some tips. It seems, though, that whenever you show up for a lesson, two or three other people are there too and you get ignored. You'd like to get to know Janelle (not to mention take advantage of the lessons), but her offer always seems to include a lot of other people. What might you do?

6. TONY was a fun friend at first, but now it seems that he doesn't want you to have any other friends. If you hang out with anybody else, he pouts and acts like you've deserted him. You like Tony, but you'd sure like to have a few other friends too. What'll you do?

Skill 13—Standing Up for Your Beliefs

INSTRUCTOR PAGE

Rationale: Standing up for something you believe in can lead to respect from others, as well as respect for yourself. Of course, some people can become obnoxious by trying to force their beliefs on others or having beliefs that are silly or don't make any sense ("I believe that I'm always right, no matter what kind of evidence you give me!"). Searching for one's values and sincerely stating those beliefs both in words and actions is an important part of getting along socially with others.

WORKSHEETS

Worksheet #69: That's Not Right!

This worksheet has a short story about a boy who stands up to two bullies on behalf of a weaker boy. Students are to respond to questions after reading the story.

Answer Key: (answers will vary)

1. belief that big people shouldn't pick on little people; 2. two bullies; 3. I like him!; 4. yes; 5. there might be a fight

Worksheet #70: What Do You Believe In?

Students are given statements of a controversial nature. They are to think about them, decide if they strongly agree or disagree with the statement, or if they simply have not given the matter any thought. Discuss why/why not and what type of evidence they would look for to help them make a decision or to sway their present decision.

Answers will vary.

Worksheet #71: Why Do You Believe That?

Students may have strong beliefs for certain reasons. On this worksheet, they are to match the character who has a strong belief with the probable reason WHY he or she feels so strongly. How can this relate to their own personal strong beliefs?

Answer Key:

1. A (father's experience); 2. D (value education); 3. B (experience of not being repaid); 4. C (taught by family); 5. E (logical)

Worksheet #72: Beliefs and Behavior

What you believe will be reflected in how you behave. On this worksheet, students are to match the character's statement with his or her probable behavior.

Answer Key:

1. E; 2. A; 3. C; 4. D; 5. B

Worksheet #73: What's the Problem?

The characters on this worksheet believe something strongly, but some of them are not on the right track. Students are to pick out the characters who have a shaky basis for their beliefs and discuss why.

Answer Key:

1. *Boy A* believes it's OK for him to go to an "R" movie; *Boy B* believes he shouldn't go if his parents wouldn't allow him to.

2. *Girl A* believes her grandmother will embarrass her; *Girl B* believes her uncle may be different but that's not a problem.

3. *Boy A* believes his best effort is good enough; *Boy B* believes copying the answers is the way to get a good grade.

4. *Girl A* believes it is OK to lie about merchandise that has been used; *Girl B* believes that is not all right.

5. *Boy A* believes Lin always wins the spelling bee; *Boy B* believes it is because her parents are rich; *Girl C* believes it is because girls are smarter than boys; *Boy D* believes she won because of her effort; and *Boy E* believes she won because of racial characteristics.

TEACHER TIPS

- In class discussions, be sure to have students give their REASONS for their opinions. Teach them to be prepared to defend their opinions. Ask for evidence or experience that supports what they say.

- As you read and discuss stories or movies, discuss what main value is represented. How do the characters show their personal beliefs?

- Talk about how beliefs are followed by actions If someone says he or she believes something but doesn't do anything to promote or defend that belief, is it a belief at all? A strong belief? Discuss how actions are often what is judged about a person first.

PARENT POINTERS

- Discuss your own personal values with your child. What is very important to you? How did you arrive at these beliefs? Which are important enough to teach to your child?

- Emphasize the importance of family as a value. Follow this by actions—spending time with your child, talking with each other, valuing each other's opinions, etc.

- As your child grows and matures, his or her values may change—and may become stronger. Let your child know when you are proud of the way he or she is taking actions to affirm the values that are becoming a part of his or her life.

PRACTICE ACTIVITIES

. . . Have students keep journal entries related to their beliefs and values. They may not want to share them with the class, but encourage them to write them down. You may include topics such as:

A Time I Took a Stand for Something—What Happened and How I Felt

What I Used to Think Was Important—and What I Think Is Important Now

Someone Who Really Affected a Belief That I Have

. . . Have students select a personal hero and research aspects of his or her life. What principles or values did (does) the hero stand for and how did (do) episodes in his or her life support this?

. . . Select a controversial topic that students may feel strongly about and have them research the opposing side. Even though they may disagree 100% with the opposition, they will learn something by finding out how someone else could possibly come up with another opinion. You might have to play the Devil's Advocate!

. . . Look for student or kid heroes in the newspaper or magazines. Every once in awhile there is a good human-interest story about things kids have done that have made a difference in some way. You may want to put these on a bulletin board and organize the beliefs and the behaviors!

That's Not Right!

Read the story about Tomas. Try to determine what is important to him and how he shows that.

Tomas walked into gym class and got ready to play basketball when he noticed Jon and Alberto, two rather large boys, teasing Frank, the class nerd. This time Jon was dangling Frank's glasses just out of his reach as the small boy desperately tried to grab them. "Jump higher, Pee Wee," Jon teased.

Tomas put his hands on his hips and shook his head. Frank was indeed an easy target. He wore thick glasses, had a speech problem, and was very small for his age. On top of that, he would rather work on a computer than catch a basketball anyday.

"Why don't you knock it off and leave him alone," Tomas demanded, stepping up to the now-increasing circle of students.

"Why don't you stay out of this?" advised Alberto, shaking a finger in Tomas's face. He gave Frank a shove, knocking him to the ground.

Tomas turned to the rest of the class that was watching with increasing interest. No one seemed to want to get too involved. "So how many of you are tired of watching these bullies harass other people?" he demanded of his audience. "Who's ready to say with me that this isn't right; enough is enough?"

At first there was a silence that seemed to last forever. Then one by one, hands went up. The two bullies looked at the vote that was taken by their peers. Every hand was up.

"You might be able to take care of one small boy," Tomas said to the bullies. "You might even be able to put me down too. But you better think carefully before you take on ALL of us."

1. What belief did Tomas stand up for?

2. Who did he stand up to?

3. How do you feel about Tomas?

4. Would you like Tomas for a friend?

5. What might happen next?

Name_____ Date _____

What Do You Believe In?

Read the following statements. Do you strongly agree with some of them? Do you strongly disagree with some? Do you feel you have no opinion or basis for judging others? Circle your response to each.

1. Sick or old people should be allowed to kill themselves if they want to. **Agree Disagree No Opinion Yet**

2. Abortion is morally wrong under any circumstance. **Agree Disagree No Opinion Yet**

3. Smoking should be illegal. **Agree Disagree No Opinion Yet**

4. No one should ever hit a child. **Agree Disagree No Opinion Yet**

5. People should not have sex until they are married. **Agree Disagree No Opinion Yet**

6. People should never shake a baby. **Agree Disagree No Opinion Yet**

7. Some drugs that are now illegal should be legalized if they will help people. **Agree Disagree No Opinion Yet**

8. If you get cancer, you will die. **Agree Disagree No Opinion Yet**

9. It's wrong to kill animals for their fur. **Agree Disagree No Opinion Yet**

10. If you can do something to make someone else's life easier, you should do it. **Agree Disagree No Opinion Yet**

11. Minority groups have a lot to offer. **Agree Disagree No Opinion Yet**

12. People shouldn't cheat on their income taxes. **Agree Disagree No Opinion Yet**

13. If you are paid in cash, you don't have to report it on your taxes. **Agree Disagree No Opinion Yet**

14. Women should not work if they have small children at home. **Agree Disagree No Opinion Yet**

15. Fourteen-year-olds should be allowed to drive. **Agree Disagree No Opinion Yet**

16. If you exercise and eat right, you will have good health the rest of your life. **Agree Disagree No Opinion Yet**

17. People with terrible scars should not go out public. **Agree Disagree No Opinion Yet**

18. College should be free and available to anyone who wants to go. **Agree Disagree No Opinion Yet**

Name_____ Date _____

Why Do You Believe That?

People have various reasons for the basis of their beliefs. Match each comment by the person on the left with the REASON why that person believes it on the right.

_____ 1. My father was an alcoholic. I remember watching him abuse my mother and other family members. Then I watched him slowly die as his liver gave out. I will never take even one drink.

_____ 2. To have lots of choices in what you do with your life, I think it's important to get a college education.

_____ 3. Sorry, I'm not going to lend you any money. The last two times I did, you never paid me back. Your excuses didn't make any sense. Sorry.

_____ 4. It's a family tradition for us to pray before meals. We have always done it, we will always do it, and when I have a family of my own, you can bet that we'll still be doing it!

_____ 5. If you take good care of your car, it will last a lot longer. Just read the maintenance manual!

A. Experience of someone you know

B. Your own experience

C. Taught by someone else

D. Something you value

E. Something that sounds logical or makes sense if you think about it

Name_____ Date _____

Beliefs and Behavior

What you believe in will affect how you act or behave. What behaviors would you expect the following people to show based on the beliefs they say they have?

1.

I believe that blind people are just like us. They enjoy many of the same things sighted people do.

2.

I believe blind people should go to special schools, not public schools.

3.

I think we should feel sorry for blind people since they are helpless.

4.

I believe restaurants should have braille menus for blind people.

5.

I believe blind people should be given every opportunity to learn and work.

A. Colleen shouldn't be here; what if she fell down the steps?

B. We're doing a science project on fossils. Here: feel this impression!

C. May I get your lunch tray for you? Here—let me help you put your coat on.

D. D-I-E-T. It's diet cola.

E. Hey, listen to this new song by Amy Grant. It's really cool!

Worksheet #73

What's the Problem?

The characters are standing up for what they believe, but what problem(s) do you see with what some of them believe?

1.

a. Hey, I know this movie is rated "R," but Joey's dad will take us. Let's go!

b. My parents don't want me to go to "R" movies. I'll join you guys later.

2.

a. I want to have some of the kids from school come over, but my grandmother only speaks German and I'm afraid she'll embarrass me.

b. My uncle from Puerto Rico is staying for a few days. He's got some interesting stories to tell. Come on over; you'll enjoy him!

3.

a. This test is really hard, but I'll do my very best.

b. Johnny has the answers to the test! If you copy them down, you'll get an A!!!

4.

a. Let's get these jeans, wear them to the party, and then take them back and say they were the wrong size. That way we won't have to pay for them.

b. That's not right. I'm not going to be a part of that!

5.

a. Lin won the spelling bee again this year. You know she always wins.

b. She won because her parents are rich.

c. She won because girls are smarter than boys.

e. NO, she won because Asians are smarter than other races.

d. She won because she studies the words and knows how to spell them.

Skill 14—Having a Good Sense of Humor

INSTRUCTOR PAGE

Rationale: What is a greater social skill than having a good sense of humor? Someone who can see the funny side of situations is possessed with a very important life skill. Someone who can learn to "lighten up" and find humor in events has truly taken a big step towards getting along with others, especially in situations in which others are not sure how to react. Someone with a good sense of humor can make a hard task fun, a dull day interesting, and can help determine others' reactions to what's going on.

WORKSHEETS

Worksheet #74: Benefits of a Sense of Humor

Students are to read the paragraphs describing how a good sense of humor can affect others and are to fill in the blanks in summary sentences.

Answer Key:

1. lighter; 2. laugh; 3. fun

Worksheet #75: Creating Humor Appropriately

Situations are listed that could have humorous overtones. Students are to think of ways in which these common situations could be funny.

Answers will vary.

Worksheet #76: Easing Tension with Humor

Students are to consider the situations on the worksheet that may have an element of tension about them. They are to think of ways in which humor could help relieve the tension.

Answers will vary.

Worksheet #77: Laughing WITH, not Laughing AT

Students are to indicate which students on the worksheet are laughing with other students and which students are laughing at other students.

Answer Key:

1. laughing with; 2. laughing at; 3. laughing at; 4. laughing with; 5. laughing with; 6. laughing with

Worksheet #78: Using Humor to Include Others

Students are to think of ways that others can be included by using humor or humorous situations.

Answers will vary.

TEACHER TIPS

- If you have a "class clown," try to use it to your advantage. Encourage him or her to use humor at appropriate times.
- Start your class with a "joke of the day" or allow students (after screening the jokes) to take a minute to tell a good, clean joke.
- Keep a few humorous posters around the room and refer to them occasionally. When you give tests, stick a cartoon at the top or bottom for students to read.
- Allow students plenty of opportunities to do skits, write plays, make videos, and interact in front of the class. Some students are natural "hams" and it's a good outlet.

PARENT POINTERS

- Keep a log of funny family moments. Record the date, events, and what happened. You might want to include photographs if they are available.

- Gather the family album or baby book and spend time with your child looking through old photos and memories. You will probably conjure up some humorous memories!

- Try using a humorous response in situations in which you normally tend to react with anger or sharpness. See what happens—besides surprising your child!

PRACTICE ACTIVITIES

. . . Give a weekly award for the student who demonstrated a good sense of humor in a situation that occurred during the week. Specify the incident!

. . . Keep a class journal of humorous experiences or moments that happen. Students will enjoy reading and remembering the events later in the year. You might have a class artist who can do a cartoon to go with the writing!

. . . After getting permission, make a class bulletin board featuring "Little Known Facts About _____" (a teacher). Perhaps Miss Santiago was a bathing beauty at age 2 and Mr. Harrison was not bald as a teenager in the sixties. Candid photos will help convey the message that the teachers have a good sense of humor.

Name_____ Date _____

Benefits of a Sense of Humor

Question: What would you do if you just discovered that you had been walking around for two hours at the mall with a white sock (straight out of the dryer) stuck on the back of your black shirt?

a. take the sock off quietly and throw it away

b. be embarrassed and ask a friend if anybody saw it

c. laugh and say, "Hey, where's the other one?"

If you picked (c), chances are you may have a good sense of humor. Having a good sense of humor means that you are able to see or find the lighter side of a situation.

A person with a good sense of humor might create humor in situations by being playful, saying funny comments that make others laugh, and not being afraid to laugh at himself or herself. A person with a good sense of humor might see a person with a broken leg and say: "Well! Some people will do anything to get out of gym." This might make the person with the broken leg feel better.

A person with a good sense of humor can laugh at himself or herself and even poke fun at his or her situation. The sock on the back of a shirt is seen as not a big deal—it's funny! The person might be embarrassed, but won't let others know or be embarrassed for him or her.

People with a sense of humor are fun to be around. They might be the class clown, causing others to laugh. Of course, even the class clown has to know when it is the right time to laugh and when to be quiet. Parties are more fun with these people around. Even if you aren't one of the people who makes others laugh, if you are one who joins in the fun and laughter, you will show that you have a good sense of humor too.

1. A person with a good sense of humor is able to see or find the _____ side of a situation.

2. A person with a good sense of humor can _____ at himself or herself.

3. People with a good sense of humor are _____ to be around.

Name_____ Date _____

Creating Humor Appropriately

What could be humorous about the following situations? Make a cartoon, role-play with others, or talk about how something could be funny without being rude or hurtful.

1. school lunches _____

_____

2. shopping with parents _____

_____

3. getting a haircut _____

_____

4. excuses for not having homework done _____

_____

5. odd relatives _____

_____

6. being late _____

_____

7. going to the dentist _____

_____

8. exercising _____

_____

9. being in a waiting room _____

_____

_____

_____

10. walking the dog _____

_____

_____

_____

Who's walking who?

Name_____ Date _____

Easing Tension with Humor

How could having a good sense of humor ease the tension in these situations? How could it help someone feel less embarrassed or included in a group?

1. You are late for your friend's surprise birthday party. When you walk in, everyone is glaring at you because you might just spoil the surprise!

2. You thought it was dress-up day at school and wore your Sunday best—while everyone else is in jeans and T-shirts.

3. Your two best friends are angry at each other and put you in the middle. Both show up at the hamburger place expecting to eat with you.

4. Your dog ran in the muddy yard and sneaked into the house—all over your mother's clean kitchen floor. To make matters worse, your company (mother's boss) is coming up the driveway now!

5. You lent some jeans to your friend and he/she accidentally got red paint all over them. He/she feels terrible! You do, too, but it's not worth getting all upset about it.

6. Your cousin is visiting and wants you to take some photos of everyone in the group. You are in charge of the camera, even though most of the time you end up cutting people's heads off when the film is developed.

7. What a klutz! You are walking through the cafeteria, past the table where the popular people sit, and trip!!! Your lunch is all over the floor!!!

8. Your science study group worked long and hard on the science fair project—only to have someone's little sister knock it over and break into pieces. No one is laughing . . .

Laughing WITH, not Laughing AT

Which of the cartoons show characters who are laughing with others in a situation? Which show characters who are laughing at others? Circle either WITH or AT.

Worksheet #78   # Using Humor to Include Others

Here are some examples of ways that others can be included by using humor. Can you think of others? Draw or write your own.

Skill 15—Using Common Sense

INSTRUCTOR PAGE

Rationale: Using common sense may seem to be an individual skill rather than a social skill, but others are still affected by one's ability or inability to think clearly and use available resources. How much time is wasted by asking others for things or information that can easily be found or answered by thinking clearly, thinking logically, or thinking harder?

WORKSHEETS

Worksheet #79: What's Common About Common Sense?

Students read the paragraphs about common sense and fill in the blanks.

Answer Key:

1. sense; 2. knowledge; resourceful; 3. clues/answers; 4. harder; 5. common sense

Worksheet #80: Looking for Clues

Charlie is a character with little common sense. Students are to look at the pictures and figure out how Charlie could easily answer his own questions without bothering anyone else.

Answer Key:

1. look at the calendar; 2. look at the directory; 3. read the note—books are not needed; 4. look at the rain outside; 5. use the map; 6. check to see if the TV is plugged in

Worksheet #81: Thinking Harder

On this worksheet, students are to consider the problems/situations and the first thought that is given to solving each. Then they are to come up with a way to solve the problem by giving each a little more thought.

Answer Key: (answers may vary)

1. go to the party, but keep your hair covered or work on your tan

2. estimate how much you will need when you start the job

3. mow your yard on Friday

4. learn to set the timer

5. get up earlier

6. find out what CDs your friend likes

Worksheet #82: Thinking Smarter

Characters on this worksheet are overlooking the obvious when dealing with their problems. Students are to identify ways that the characters can handle their problems by thinking smarter.

Answer Key:

1. take the bike off; 2. eat a small snack; 3. shut the door; 4. write it down

Worksheet #83: Using Your Common Sense

Each situation on this worksheet portrays a character who is not using common sense or who is in a situation in which they need to do something that requires common sense. Students are to make suggestions.

Answer Key: (answers may vary)

1. pay the book rental; there will be other sales

2. wait until after the move to start such a big project

3. magic markers don't erase; David needs to use a pencil

4. Justine should get her cat spayed

5. they should take water bottles with them

6. Carmine needs to practice more, not just before his lesson

7. Antonio needs to take sunscreen

8. she could call her mother at home to bring her running shoes

TEACHER TIPS

- Don't give students the answers to their questions too quickly. Instead, give them clues or hints and enough response time that they can try to develop a response on their own.

- To help students take responsibility for their daily work and homework, have students plan their own schedule for studying before a test. Emphasize using common sense and knowledge about studying strategies. You may have them keep track of the time spent in active studying and their earned grade.

PARENT POINTERS

- Instead of telling your child what to do ("You better wash your gym clothes tonight!"), use questions to help direct your child to make choices ("What could happen if you wait until the morning to wash your gym clothes? Is there a way to be better prepared?")

- Some children who are not academically skilled have a lot of common sense. Look for ways to praise your child and give him or her opportunities to use this knowledge and ability. Be sure to use the phrase "common sense."

- When a child makes a poor choice or mistake, try not to yell at or belittle him or her. Instead, turn the situation into a lesson. "Well, that didn't work. What might be a better way to handle this the next time?" Then use the information for future use. "We sure won't lock the keys in the car again! Now we'll remember to keep a spare set. That problem is taken care of!"

PRACTICE ACTIVITIES

. . . Post a Question of the Day on your board that requires using common sense to answer. Make sure that everything needed to solve the problem or answer the question is somewhere in the room. Examples: How many days are left in this month? (check the calendar) Who has birthdays in October? (check the birthday board) In what classes will there be tests on Friday? (check the posted assignment sheet) Students will enjoy taking turns making up the daily questions!!

. . . When in a public place such as a mall or grocery store, have students listen to the way parents talk to their small children. What examples of common sense do they hear? ("Don't walk in the mud; you'll get your new shoes dirty.")

. . . Some comedy is based on characters who have little or no common sense (dumb blonde/The Three Stooges/absent-minded professors). Have students watch and analyze television shows that portray these types of characters. Why do we find this so funny?

. . . Students may be amused by looking through some tabloids to find outrageous stories that are reported. Again, analyze why they may defy common sense! (Elvis? Aliens? Animals having human babies?)

. . . Have students draw comics or pictures containing something illogical in it. After exchanging or displaying the pictures, have students try to identify what's wrong or illogical with each. Ideas might include having someone set out some ice cubes to take to school tomorrow, someone traveling to the sun "at night" when it's cooler, a drawing of a book with the title on the back cover instead of the front cover, etc.

Name_____ Date _____

What's Common About Common Sense?

Most people put their socks on before they put their shoes on. Why? Well, think about it! Some things don't make any sense when you stop to think them through. Why should you wear a coat outside when it's 10 degrees below zero? Why wouldn't you drink a cola with a lot of caffeine in it before going to bed? It seems to be obvious when you think about. That's what common sense is all about—just using ordinary knowledge or being resourceful to solve a problem. Nothing special. Nothing out of the ordinary. Just common things that most people know and common thinking that most people can do.

Many problems can be solved by looking for clues that will give an answer—clues that are right in front of you. If your car ran out of gas in front of a 24-hour gas station . . . well, what would be an obvious thing to do? The answer may be right in front of you.

Another way to use common sense is by thinking harder about something. Let's go back to the car that ran out of gas. Take away the gas station. Now you'll have to think a little harder to figure out what to do. Would you go walking down the highway with a paper bag to put some gas in? Would you use your car phone to call your mother in another state to come and help you out? Hey! If you have a car phone, what's another possibility for you? Think harder!

There are many people who have common sense. They are good thinkers. They look for clues. They think harder when an idea is not right in front of them. Answers are all around you! Now find them!

1. Some things don't make any _____ when you think them through.

2. Common sense is just using ordinary _____ or being _____ when solving a problem.

3. Many problems can be solved by looking for _____ that are right in front of you.

4. Another way to use common sense to solve problems is to think _____ about them.

5. Many people who are good thinkers have _____ .

Name_____ Date _____

Looking for Clues

Help Charlie use common clues to answer his own questions.

Name_____ Date _____

Thinking Harder

How could you solve the problems or deal with these situations by thinking harder?

| **Situations** | | **Thinking Harder** |

1. You can't get your hair wet for 24 hours after you get it permed. You got your hair permed today. You are invited to a pool party tomorrow.

   First Thought: skip the party

_____
_____
_____

2. You are painting your garage. You buy a small can and plan to use it up first. You aren't sure how much paint you'll need.

   First Thought: keep going back for more paint when you run out

_____
_____
_____

3. You need to mow your yard. The weather report for Saturday calls for rain. It's Friday morning and it's sunny.

   First Thought: hope that the report is wrong

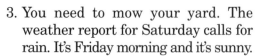

_____
_____
_____

4. You want to tape your favorite TV show on a videotape, but you have to leave.

   First Thought: you ask a friend if he'll come over and turn on the VCR right before the show

_____
_____
_____

5. You have an early-morning meeting tomorrow.

   First Thought: you know you'll have to move faster in the morning

_____
_____
_____

6. You want to buy a birthday present for a friend. You know she likes CDs and has a CD player.

   First Thought: pick out a CD *you* like

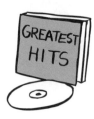

_____
_____
_____

Name_____ Date _____

Thinking Smarter

How could the characters below think smarter to solve their problems?

1.

2.

3.

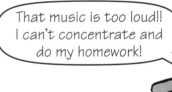

4.

Name_____ Date _____

Using Your Common Sense

What's wrong with each situation below? How could using common sense help come up with a solution?

1. Arnold owes $63 for book rentals, but he finds a pair of jeans on sale and wants to use the money to buy them since the sale ends tomorrow.

2. Carla is moving across the country to a new state. The day before the move, she wants to start putting together a 1,000-piece puzzle on the kitchen table.

3. The teacher asked David to do his math in pencil since she is teaching a new concept and the students will probably make mistakes. David pulls out his black magic marker.

4. Justine's cat roams all over the neighborhood and has just had its third litter of kittens. Justine knows she will have trouble finding homes for the kittens.

5. Paulina and Dustin are planning to go on an all-day bike ride out into the country. It's going to be really hot and sunny on the day they go.

6. Carmine takes piano lessons every Thursday after school. He practices on Wednesday for 5 minutes. He doesn't understand why he never seems to be getting any better!

7. Antonio is invited to a pool party on a hot day. He has fair skin and burns easily.

8. Kara has track practice after school, but she left her running shoes at home. She decides to borrow her friend's shoes, even though they are a little too small for her.

Skill 16—Developing a Good Reputation

INSTRUCTOR PAGE

Rationale: Having a good reputation is one of the most important—and valuable—things a person can possess. It is helpful information to know what one's reputation is, to think about what qualities are valued, and to make positive efforts towards achieving a good reputation.

WORKSHEETS

Worksheet #84: What Others Say About You

Students are given the opportunity to consider the opinions about "Ted," a character with definite qualities.

Answer Key:

1. a very good reputation; from all sources

2. no—too many people seem to vouch for his honesty and other characteristics

3. they seem to—Ted must be consistent in his living and conversation

4. probably

Worksheet 85: Developing a Reputation

This worksheet contains a list of some of the ways people develop a reputation. Students are to discuss how each of them can contribute to developing someone's reputation.

Answer Key: (answers will vary)

1. people might assume you are similar in many ways to the people you hang around with

2. your activities give clues as to what you are interested in

3. the words you say reflect what you're thinking about

4. if you appear pleasant, people might assume you are!

5. if you're unkind to others, you may get a reputation as being self-centered or unthoughtful

6. outgoing people might be perceived as friendlier or more desirable to know than quiet people

Worksheet #86: Misjudging Others

Students are to discuss reputations that might be misleading or how a person might be misjudged.

Answer Key: (answers will vary)

1. many quiet people might be misjudged as being snobs when they are really just shy

2. this boy doesn't really know Mark at all; he's making judgments based on hearsay

3. this person thinks the girl is a poor student simply because she's poor

4. this girl hasn't invested any time in learning about Charlie, who actually has some fantastic creative abilities

Worksheet #87: What's Your Reputation?

Students should be reflective on this worksheet. They are to think about what people who are close to them might say about their reputation.

Answers will vary.

Worksheet #88: What Kind of Reputation Do You Want?

This page contains adjectives that may or may not describe each student. Students are to circle those they wish others would use when talking about their reputation.

Answer Key: (answers will vary)

Worksheet #89: Changing Your Reputation

Changing one's reputation is a difficult process, but it can happen. On this worksheet, students are to think of ways a reputation can be changed.

Answer Key: (answers will vary)

1. start joining other activities

2. resolve to only say positive things about others

3. volunteer to tutor kids after school

4. be the first to donate to the fund to help feed hungry children; better yet, start the fund

5. practice a few general opening lines

6. put forth extra effort to be trustworthy around your parents

TEACHER TIPS

- Help build up your students' reputation by informing them of their good qualities as situations come up. A kind, sincere word from a teacher goes a long way. They will remember what kind of reputation you are giving them. "You are always on time." "I can always count on you to have a creative slant to things!"

- Use the term *reputation* in your discussions of manufacturers, products, places, resorts, and other things. Talk about how reputations can make a difference in what kind of car you buy, what type of dog you own, where you go out to eat, and so on.

- Teachers, too, gain reputations—some for being too tough, really funny, easy-going, caring, giving too much work, etc. Talk about how the different roles people play can affect their reputation. Do we assume a football coach must be loud, active, and confrontational?

PARENT POINTERS

- Ask your child to tell you about some of the students in school who have "good" reputations and "bad" reputations. What specific qualities are assigned to each? Is it considered "out" or unpopular to be smart? athletic? kind?

- Refer to the reputation of someone or something as daily activities come up. Discuss why you would choose one doctor over another based on reputation. Help your child see the importance that having a good reputation has in lots of areas.

PRACTICE ACTIVITIES

. . . Discuss the reputation of entertainers, athletes, well-known political figures, and other celebrities. How did they get their reputations? Do you think they are truly deserved? Is one incident enough for a reputation to start growing in a certain direction?

. . . Bring in political cartoons that show caricatures of well-known individuals. Discuss how these exaggerated attributes tie in to someone's reputation.

. . . Have students keep a journal with entries including: (a) What characteristics do you feel are important for having a good reputation? (b) What do you think your reputation is right now? (c) Who are some people with good reputations that you admire? (d) Was there ever a time when you had a bad reputation? How did you deal with it and what did you do to try to change it?

. . . Collect magazine ads or analyze television commercials in terms of how a reputation can influence or affect the image. Are Maytags® really reliable? Can Tide® get out all of those stains? Do the builders of a Saturn car really care about you?

Name_____ Date _____

What Others Say About You

Meet Ted. Here is what others have to say about Ted. Think about what kind of reputation he has.

TED'S GIRLFRIEND, MARIE: Ted has the best sense of humor of anyone I know. I thing that's what I enjoy most about him—the way he can take an ordinary situation and see what is funny about it.

TED'S BEST FRIEND, ANDRE: If you're on a team, you want to be on Ted's side, that's for sure! He plays so seriously—there's no goofing around if you're playing with him. But he wants everyone to play fair. No cheating!

TED'S BOSS: Ted has worked here at the gas station for about six months now. He works part-time during school and full-time in the summer. Ted will give you your money's worth—he never cheats on his time card and he is always willing to work overtime. He's one of the few employees who I don't have to constantly supervise to make sure he's working.

TED'S TEACHER: I am so proud of Ted. Chemistry is not always easy, but Ted gives his best. He might not get A's and B's on everything, but I know what he turns in is his own work. He's not afraid to ask questions if he doesn't understand something, either. When something is due, he turns it in on time. I really appreciate that!

TED'S FATHER: Ted takes on a lot of responsibility around the house, I guess since he is the oldest and his mother and I both work a lot of extra hours. He often has to look after his younger brother and sister, and that means driving them to their activities sometimes when he would probably rather be doing something else.

1. What kind of reputation does Ted have?

2. If someone else told you that Ted was a liar and a cheater, would you tend to believe them? Why or why not?

3. Do you think all of these people who know Ted have the same impression about him? Why?

4. Is Ted someone you would like to know?

Name_____ Date _____

Developing a Reputation

How do the following people or situations help you develop a reputation?

1. who you hang around with

_____

_____

_____

2. the activities you participate in

_____

_____

_____

3. what you talk about

_____

_____

_____

4. how you appear to others

_____

_____

_____

5. how you treat other people

_____

_____

_____

6. your personality

_____

_____

_____

_____

Name_____   Date _____

Worksheet #86

Misjudging Others

Before you form an opinion about someone, you might want to make sure you're being objective and aren't just seeing what you want to see. How did each character change a misjudged opinion in the following situations?

The Snob

Kari is so stuck up. She doesn't talk to anyone, she just keeps to herself, and won't join in anything.

Maybe you don't know that Kari's really shy. She's very smart, but usually she's afraid to talk in class.

The Genius

I heard that Mark has an IQ of 300 or something like that. He's always doing science stuff in his garage. I think he's building an invention.

Mark is good at building things, but I don't think he's a genius. He's good at science, but I think he's just an average student in everything else.

The Dummy

Have you seen the dirty clothes that Maggie wears? She's absent from school about twice a week. I think she's flunking everything.

Maggie comes from a very poor family. She's sick a lot, and that's why she misses so much school. Her whole family needs a lot of help.

The Bore

Charlie is so dull. He doesn't play any sports or seem to have any interests. He's so quiet in school—he never says much. No wonder he doesn't have any friends.

You should see the fantastic paintings Charlie draws in his basement. Someone from a Chicago art school has talked to him about enrolling next year. He's really creative!!

What's Your Reputation?

What do you think the following people would say or tell about you if asked about your reputation?

Your mother . . . _____
_____
_____

Your father . . . _____
_____
_____

Your neighbor . . . _____
_____
_____

Your best friend . . . _____
_____
_____

A classmate . . . _____
_____
_____

A brother or sister . . . _____
_____
_____

A teacher . . . _____
_____
_____

Your boss or someone you have worked for . . . _____
_____
_____

Another adult (specify) . . . _____
_____
_____

Name_____ Date _____

What Kind of Reputation
Do You Want?

Think about what you wish people would say about you or think of you. Circle some of the words below that you wish would describe your reputation. You may add to the list!

kind	thoughtful	outgoing	greedy
truthful	loyal	fun	happy
hard-working	creative	easy to fool	athletic
fair	careful	good cook	gets good grades
class clown	easily bored	quiet	life of the party
easily amused	lots of interests	good listener	smart
shares	thinks of others	finishes things	clever

Other words that describe me:

_____
_____
_____
_____
_____
_____
_____
_____
_____
_____
_____

Name_____ Date _____

Changing Your Reputation

Let's say you wanted to change your reputation. What are some things you could do?

1. You have a reputation as being a bookworm. You really want people to know you have a lot of interests besides books, such as sports and acting.

_____

2. You hate it, but you must admit—you're a gossip. Whenever you hear something interesting but negative about someone, you can't wait to tell everyone else. And everyone comes to you for information, knowing that you know and you'll tell. But you've had enough. You've decided to quit being a gossip.

_____

3. You're a wonderful basketball player—but people assume because you're a good athlete you're not very smart. Actually, you're a decent student but people seem to overlook that.

_____

4. Your parents have taught you to be careful with your money. You are, but perhaps it's a little extreme. You find yourself pulling out a calculator all the time, making sure you don't pay more than your fair share, ever. Your friends are getting annoyed, and you think you should rethink being too tight with your money.

_____

5. You're so shy it hurts! You really envy people who can walk into a room full of strangers and start talking comfortably. You want to become a better conversationalist.

_____

6. You're one of the POPULAR kids! Lucky you! But you've heard that because the popular kids you hang around with have gotten into some minor trouble with the police, your name is brought up, too. Your parents are starting to ask you a lot of questions and always want to know where you are going and who you're with—as if they don't trust you anymore.

_____

Skill 17—Reacting Appropriately to Peer Pressure

INSTRUCTOR PAGE

Rationale: Pressure from peers is very strong and can be positive or negative, depending on how it affects one's personal stance and goals. Students need to realize how powerful this pressure can be and be equally strong in their decisions as to how to respond to it.

WORKSHEETS

Worksheet #90: Feeling the Pressure

Students are given a short story about two characters who experience pressure—one positive (to join in a sport) and the other negative (to be cruel to someone).

Answer Key:

1. positive pressure

2. negative pressure

3. Nancy may have learned that joining in can be fun; Robbie may have learned that it isn't worth hurting others to be accepted by another group.

Worksheet #91: Positive and Negative Peer Pressure

Students are to read a list of comments that reflect either a positive or negative perspective.

Answer Key:

1. positive; 2. positive; 3. negative; 4. positive; 5. negative; 6. positive; 7. negative; 8. positive; 9. negative; 10. positive; 11. negative; 12. negative; 13. positive; 14. negative; 15. positive; 16. negative

Worksheet #92: Everybody's Doing It

Even if a peer group gives approval to an activity, it does not necessarily mean that it is okay for an individual in a different situation.

Answer Key:

1. *positive*—time spent with a friend; *negative*—maybe time should be spent studying or getting ready for the day

2. *positive*—the "right" running shoes are important for a serious athlete; *negative*—the person may not be able to afford or even need expensive shoes

3. *negative*—could be harmful; *neutral*—may not matter

4. *negative*—could be harmful

5. *positive*—could be exciting and fun; *negative*—may try to get someone to do something he or she does not really want to do

6. *negative*—could get caught and get in trouble

7. *positive*—may have a humorous idea for your license plate; *negative*—may not want to spend the extra money

8. *negative*—sounds like this person has tried to lose weight before; this person may really be criticizing the other

9. *negative*—that's a lot of money to spend for a dress

10. *negative*—now the pressure is on to spend a lot of money on a limo and the prom

11. *positive*—perhaps Mr. Jones will think it's funny; *negative*—perhaps Mr. Jones will be upset

12. *negative*—this is vandalism

Worksheet #93: Why We Respond to Peers

This worksheet gives examples of why peer pressure is so powerful. Students are to match the reasons with the examples.

Answer Key:

1. b (member of the track team)
2. e (the weird hairstyle is accepted by the others)
3. d (they all feel the same way about study time)
4. c (peers can fulfill a friendship role)
5. a (you might try things you wouldn't think of trying on your own)
6. f (being smart is accepted by this group)

Worksheet #94: When There's a Conflict

Students are to think about their position in a conflict situation by considering the following questions: Is it a question of right and wrong? Could this be harmful? How will it affect my long-range goals?

Answer Key: (answers may vary)

1. take Japanese—it's part of her long-range goals
2. this person may feel that it's wrong for him to use a fake ID to go to a movie that is not appropriate for him
3. could be harmful
4. may affect long-range goals
5. could be harmful
6. question of right/wrong

Worksheet #95: Resisting Negative Pressure

This worksheet contains a list of ways to help deal with negative peer pressure. Students are to think of ways they could apply them to their own situations.

Answers will vary.

TEACHER TIPS

- You are in a position to observe peer pressure and its effects first-hand. Talk about how individuals who stand up for themselves, their values, their reputations, and their beliefs have a perfect right to stand up to pressure that negatively affects them.

- Identify the social outcasts in your class. Do what you can to enhance their skills and talents among peers. Try to find the uniquenesses of each student and highlight them whenever possible.

- Make your rules clear when you use cooperative groups. Everyone must participate, courtesy among members is expected, the team must produce a product, etc.

- Many students of this age have poor self concepts. Use every opportunity to preach the message of valuing yourself over and over and over.

PARENT POINTERS

- Realize that peers have a powerful influence on your child—and it's not necessarily all negative. Seek out the positive effects and encourage them (joining groups, taking risks, becoming more vocal in their beliefs and discoveries, etc.).

- Reaffirm your family's values and expectations. Be clear with your child about what you expect of him or her in terms of school, leisure time, home responsibilities, etc. Remember that your family is Your Family and follow its rules which may not be the same as others (e.g., "We do homework after school every school night before we go out with friends," etc.).

- Discuss consequences of breaking rules with your child. Have a family meeting regularly to keep lines of communication open and to talk specifically about rules and limits, and when it is appropriate to make changes in them, depending on your trust in your child and his or her ability to adhere to the existing rules.

- Find out who your child's peers are and what the pressures are in your child's life. Are drugs a problem? Does your child feel inferior? Check in occasionally with the teacher, school counselor, and other parents.

PRACTICE ACTIVITIES

. . . Dig out old fashion magazines from 20 to 30 years ago and have a good laugh. Then talk about how things that were popular back then have changed (and come back in a different form). Specifically, look at hairstyles, clothing, fads, language, music, dances, and social concerns. What's the same today? What's different? Was there more pressure back then? Or just different pressure?

. . . Get pen-pals from another section of the country and exchange information on what's popular or trendy there. Is peer pressure the same across different parts of the country?

. . . Conduct a survey. What are the Top Ten pressures felt by students at the school? This could lead to a good discussion on ways to handle the pressure, individually or as a school.

Feeling the Pressure

Nancy sat nervously on the edge of the bench as she waited for the softball game to begin. She always enjoyed watching her friends play, especially because they usually won.

"Hey, Nancy," called Angela as she jogged past her. "Why don't you join us? Caroline got sick and we could use another player to take her place."

"Oh, no," Nancy cried, shaking her head. "I'm no good. You'd be better off playing with fewer players."

"No, join us!" insisted Janine. "It's all just for fun. We don't care if we win or lose. Oops, there's the coach. Pretend you didn't hear me say that!" They all laughed.

"Well . . . I'm not sure," Nancy moaned, protesting as the girls grabbed each of her arms and tried dragging her over to where the teams were gathering. "I guess I could . . . just this once."

Meanwhile, Robbie was behind the bleachers with several of his friends, waiting for the game to begin. "We'll give you five dollars to trip Nancy as she walks by," Travis offered to Robbie. "It'll be really funny."

"I don't really want to," Robbie said. He knew what it was like to be the object of a joke and to be laughed at.

"Oh, come on," Arnie said, slapping Robbie on the back. "We'll stand on each side of you. Then when she walks by, just stick your leg out. Make it look like an accident."

"I don't know," Robbie said. "I don't think it's very nice . . ."

"Here she comes," Arnie whispered, shoving Robbie in front of him. "Do it."

"Well, OK," Robbie said. He knocked into Nancy and watched sadly as she tripped and fell face first to the ground. Nancy picked herself up and stared at Robbie. Robbie couldn't look at her. Instead, he looked around for his friends. Where did they go? Suddenly he was the center of attention—and felt very stupid.

1. What kind of peer pressure did Nancy experience?

2. What kind of peer pressure did Robbie experience?

3. What do you think Nancy and Robbie learned from their experiences with doing what their peers wanted them to do?

Positive and Negative Peer Pressure

Read each of the comments below. Decide which show pressure from peers to do something positive and place a *P* on the appropriate lines. Place an *N* next to the comments that show pressure from peers to do something negative.

_____ 1. "Let's join 4-H. It'll be really fun."

_____ 2. "We're all going to go to the spring dance. I know we have to invite girls, but if we all do it, it'll be ok."

_____ 3. "Everyone smokes. Here—I've got a whole pack for you."

_____ 4. "If you got your hair cut like Hannah's, your face would really show. I know where you can get it cut."

_____ 5. "If you want to be accepted, you'd better swear once in awhile or people will think you're goody-goody."

_____ 6. "Volunteering at the hospital is a really neat experience. We can sign up after school to work there all summer."

_____ 7. "Don't talk to Debbie. We're all mad at her because she acts like she's better than we are."

_____ 8. "They're having a sale on sweatpants at the sporting goods store. We're going to wear them with our favorite baseball team shirts on Friday."

_____ 9. "If a cop tries to pull me over and give me a ticket, I'll tell him a thing or two. Don't let them boss you around."

_____ 10. "Our group is meeting tonight to cook a Russian meal for an extra-credit project for Social Studies. Join us."

_____ 11. "If anyone thinks they can beat me up, you're welcome to try it right now."

_____ 12. "Don't buy those cheap jeans—they look awful. If you don't have expensive jeans, you'll get talked about."

_____ 13. "I don't think you should go out with Brent. He's got a really bad reputation and I know he's been in trouble with the police. I would worry about you."

_____ 14. "I know your parents don't want you to get a tattoo, but I know where you can get one really cheap. They'll never find out."

_____ 15. "We're collecting money to send to an orphanage in Haiti. We're trying to get 100% participation for our class. Can you donate?"

_____ 16. "You can finish your homework later—we are all going to the movies tonight. Come on."

Everybody's Doing It

Even if "everyone is doing it," are the effects of joining in positive, negative, or just neutral (doesn't really matter)? How could the same example be positive for someone and negative for someone else?

1. *Let's get to school early so we can walk around and talk.*

_____
_____

2. *You better get expensive running shoes.*

_____
_____

3. *Come on—let's get our noses pierced!*

_____
_____

4. *Smoking is okay as long as you don't inhale.*

_____
_____

5. *We're all going skydiving next weekend!*

_____
_____

6. *We can stay out past the curfew if we don't get caught.*

_____
_____

7. *For an extra $10, you can get a personalized license plate for your car.*

_____
_____

8. *You would look really great if you lost another ten pounds. Are you going to try to get really skinny again?*

_____
_____

9. *That dress you really liked is on sale for only $500!!! Please get it!*

_____
_____

10. *Well, you and Tony are going to the prom in a stretch limo, aren't you?*

_____
_____

11. *Let's toilet paper Mr. Jones's house! He'll think it's really funny!*

_____
_____

12. *Get your baseball bat—we can knock down some mailboxes while we're driving!*

_____
_____

Name_____ Date _____

Why We Respond to Peers

Why are peers and peer approval so important to us? Match the reason on the left with the example on the right.

_____ **1.** Being part of a peer group gives us an identity.

_____ **2.** Being part of a peer group gives a feeling of safety and acceptance.

_____ **3.** There is strength in numbers—when many peers make a statement, people listen.

_____ **4.** It's nice to have friends or people to do things with.

_____ **5.** It can be exciting!

_____ **6.** Most people don't want to be thought of as "odd" or singled out for being different.

Name_____ Date _____

When There's a Conflict

Sometimes you may not agree with or feel comfortable with the type of pressure that peers are putting on you. Think about:

- Does this involve a question of right vs. wrong?
- Could this be harmful to me?
- How will this affect my long-range goals for myself?

How might you resolve the following conflicts?

1.
   Oh, take French for a foreign language. We're all taking French. Then we can talk to each other!
   But I wanted to take Japanese. I hope to go to Japan as an exchange student.

2.
   Come on—let's go to the XXX movie! We can get fake IDs!
   I don't even want to go to that movie—but I don't want to be the only one who isn't going...

3.
   Here—take a cigarette. You'll look funny if you aren't smoking. You want to be cool, don't you?
   Do I?

4.
   Oh, come on—don't be so old-fashioned! All of the girls I go out with like to have sex. And if you get pregnant, don't worry. There are all kinds of things you can do now to take care of that!
   Why is he making all of these decisions for me? I'm planning on college, not motherhood!

5.
   I'm so terrified I can't talk.
   I wonder how fast I can take this curve! Hang on! Wheeeeeeee!!

6.
   If you tell on us, we'll come after you! Think about it!!
   I don't want any part of this—but no one would believe me!

© 1998 by John Wiley & Sons, Inc.

Name_____ Date _____

Resisting Negative Pressure

Here are some ways you can resist negative peer pressure. How could you use these in situations that have happened to you?

1. Find a source of strength (counselor, best friend, religion).

2. Find new friends who share your values.

3. Think of your long-range goals—don't lose sight of them.

4. Put the situation in perspective: Will this matter 10 years from now?

5. Get deeply involved in something positive (volunteer work, getting straight A's on your report card, sports, choir, etc.),

6. Decide to value yourself. Is it worth it to you and your reputation to give in to the pressure? Is it worth fighting?

7. Use humor to get out of the situation.

8. Don't waver in your stand: NO means NO. Practice saying it until it comes naturally!

9. Think about your reputation and what you want it to be.

10. Be a peer who puts positive pressure on others (encourage others to join you in your quests, include others in your activities, be a leader, etc.).

Skill 18—Making Good Decisions

INSTRUCTOR PAGE

Rationale: Making decisions usually involves other people. When we make good decisions, it can affect other people in a positive way. Making poor decisions can cause harm and pain to others (e.g., parents, children, family members, etc.). It is often difficult to make decisions, especially when a lot is at stake. However, by having and using a common-sense strategy for making decisions, individuals may be able to clarify what is important to everyone involved.

WORKSHEETS

Worksheet #96: Questions to Ask Yourself

This worksheet details some questions that can be helpful in narrowing down what information is important to make a good decision.

Answer Key:

1. minor or trivial; 2. decision; 3. reversed; 4. urgent, time; 5. guides, relationship

Worksheet #97: A Decision-Making Chart

This chart shows some logical steps involved in making decisions. Questions that can lead to eliminating some options or the realization that more information is needed help guide the learner through a process for making decisions.

Answers will vary.

Worksheet #98: What Decision Needs to Be Made?

The student is to select the most obvious decision that needs to be made in the situations listed on the worksheet. Then, by using the decision-making chart and its questions, the student can go through the process of helping to make a good decision appropriate for the situation.

Answer Key:

1. deciding what treatment is most appropriate for the dog—putting her down? trying more medication?
2. deciding what treatment is most appropriate for Grandma—should she go to a nursing home? visiting nurse? receive more/different medication?
3. deciding what you will do after high school—work? vocational training? college?
4. deciding whether or not to buy the house—more information is needed about the cost, payments, etc.
5. Janelle needs to decide whether or not marriage is truly the best option for her
6. deciding where to take the vacation
7. deciding how quickly you can get medical treatment
8. deciding whether to call the police or get further information about the noise
9. deciding what to do about feeding everybody
10. deciding whether or not to go to school, take the test, ask for more time, etc.

Worksheet #99: Trivial vs. Important

Students are to decide whether or not the decision facing each character on the worksheet is trivial or important—and give a basis for their decision.

Answer Key:

1. trivial—doesn't affect anyone else
2. important—affects many people
3. important—affects the quality of life of the lady
4. important to the girl who is getting married; possibly trivial to anyone else

5. important to the student making the decision; to anyone who is not in the class

6. possibly important (if the man is a legitimate agent); possibly trivial since the likelihood of the boy becoming a huge star is minimal

7. important—the girl may obtain a scholarship

Worksheet #100: When You Need More Information

In each case, further information is needed to help make a good decision. Students are to come up with examples of the type of information necessary or helpful.

Answer Key: (answers may vary)

1. how secure his present job is; if he can afford the payments (plus the insurance)

2. the difference in price between the flights; how much time is spent waiting for (and between) planes

3. what kind of computer you can afford; what options/programs you may need

4. what kind of person Mark is; what Mark looks like; Mark's interests

5. how much time is involved in each sport; whether you are more skilled at one over the other

6. if you plan to need history credits for college; other opinions about Mr. Peters as a teacher

7. how much the insurance costs; how you will obtain the money

8. what you have to do to earn the money; if you have to put money up front before you get paid; if this is a legitimate business proposition

Worksheet #101: Decisions That Affect Other People

After considering the decisions the individuals have made, the student should think about how it will affect other people.

Answer Key: (answers may vary)

1. the dentist decided to become a specialist for children—people who are afraid of dentists will probably take their children to him

2. Mr. Smith has decided to put his job and his drinking over his children—time with them and their needs

3. the professor has decided to put little effort into class—as a result his students will probably learn very little

4. Karen has decided to become an excellent nurse—her patients will receive the benefit of her attitude and treatment

5. Markie will probably make a lot of mistakes on the job—as a result he will have to answer for many customer complaints

6. Jan will probably receive many referrals for doing weddings

7. the salesman will probably not have many repeat customers

8. the contractor will probably receive a lot of complaints on his work

9. the coach will probably have a lot of players who respect her and her rules

10. the basketball player will probably receive a lot of praise and have a big ego, but he is not a team player and may not be chosen for a college team

Worksheet #102: Head vs. Heart Decisions

Some decisions that work out well can be made impulsively or "by instinct"; however, using common sense might better steer you towards a good decision. Students are to consider possible problems with the impulsive decisions on the worksheet.

Answer Key: (answers may vary)

1. the shares of stock may lose value

2. later the girl may decide that a secure person would have made her life easier

3. the puppy is against the rules, will probably bark and get her into trouble, and will outgrow the size of the small apartment

4. the person will end up paying a lot of extra money on interest charges

5. the person may not want to put forth the extra work to become a doctor, but later may wish that he or she could help children's medical needs; also the difference in pay may later be a consideration

6. the girl may wish she had gotten some money for the tickets

TEACHER TIPS

- Emphasize the concept of COST of a decision. What is a consequence of not doing your homework, cheating on a test, choosing to study with a partner rather than alone, etc.?

- Every decision has some sort of price tag. Discuss the cost of a professional athlete's decision to play for a team, an actor's price to pay for fame, a politician's lack of a normal personal life, etc.

- When possible, give students opportunities to make decisions that will affect their grades, reports, creative activities to complete class assignments, etc. You might find that students will work themselves harder than you would have!

- If a student chooses to be a behavior problem or a class clown, inform him or her that a decision has just been made that affects the whole class. Lead the class into a discussion of how interruptions cost the class time, freedom of options, and lack of focus.

PARENT POINTERS

- Give your child practice in making decisions for him- or herself whenever possible. Help your child to label decisions with terms such as trivial, important, urgent, requiring more information, cost, consequences, etc.

- Let your child know that you are available as a nonjudgmental sounding board for making decisions. Don't be too quick to make decisions for your child; instead help to guide him or her through the common-sense questions of narrowing down a decision.

- If your child makes a "bad" decision, try to help him or her find the point of where it broke down. Did he or she forget about how many people were involved? Decide that it was a lesson learned and leave it at that!

- Observe your child's style of decision-making: practical? impulsive? thoughtful? painstakingly slow? Do you model any of these attributes? Are there better alternatives?

PRACTICE ACTIVITIES

. . . Have students make a list of decisions that they typically made during a day/week/month/year/decade, etc. Rate them according to major/minor, urgency, cost, risk, others involved, etc.

. . . Give students situations to think about in order to come up with a group (or individual) decision. For example, pretend that they have just been given $20,000 to buy a car. They must do some research to find the best buy for their money. Remind them to go through advantages and disadvantages of various types of cars. Need or purpose of the car is also an important consideration here!

. . . How are important decisions made on high levels such as the government or presidency? (Cabinet members, etc.) What could contribute to decisions about foreign policy? What about local decisions? Who makes those and who influences those decisions?

. . . Have students interview some adults to find out about some decisions they made that were regretted or mistakes as well as those that turned out to be risky but wonderful.

Name_____ Date _____

Questions to Ask Yourself

Think of all the decisions you make in a day! Will you have cereal or donuts for breakfast? Will you have time for breakfast at all? Should you wear black jeans or blue? Get to class early or hang out in the hall in hopes of accidentally-on-purpose running into someone special? Go to a movie or clean your room? (Well . . . some decisions are more obvious than others!) Throughout the day you are faced with lots of decisions to make.

Here are some questions to ask yourself that might make it easier to come to a decision:

- **How important is this decision?** Some decisions are relatively minor and don't make a lot of difference. The color of your clothes or what movie you see may not have a long-term impact on your life past that day. However, other decisions are very important and can affect the course of your life. Decisions affecting what you'll be doing after high school, choosing a college or vocation, getting a job, getting married, deciding where you'll live, whether or not to buy a house, having children and . . . wow! It never stops!

- **How does your decision affect others?** If you break up with Wally, are all of his friends going to snub you? If you go against your parents' wishes because you don't want to go to law school, will they cut you out of the will? If you join one group, does that exclude joining another group? If you decide you're not going to drive your friends to Florida over spring break (and you're the one with the car), how will that affect your relationship with your friends? And what if you decide to give the $10,000 from Aunt Jane to the local animal shelter in memory of Buffy the kitty instead of going to college—how will that affect Aunt Jane?

- **Is the decision reversible?** If you choose one path—for example, going to the community college and working for a year instead of borrowing the money to go to Harvard—could you still end up at your goal of completing college? You may be able to take a risk if you have a good backup plan. But first think through the consequences. Can you live with your choice if you're stuck with it?

- **How urgent is the decision?** Do you have to make a life-and-death call right now? Call 911? Buy the car while it's on sale? Choose an experimental drug to treat a disease? Get the puppy or the adult dog? We all have to make decisions within a certain time frame, and knowing those time limits can help decide the urgency.

- **Finally, what guides you in making the decision?** Is your decision consistent with your values? Does it help get you toward your goals or something that you need? Is it helpful for many people, rather than a selfish venture for yourself? Decisions are based in a large part on your values, goals, needs, and relationship with other people.

1. Some decisions are relatively _____ and don't make a big difference in your life. Others, however, are very important.

2. You should also think about how your _____ will affect other people.

3. Some decisions can be _____ ; that is, you can change your mind if you want to.

4. If a decision is very _____ , you might have to make a decision right away. On the other hand, sometimes you can take your _____ making up your mind.

5. Finally, you should decide what _____ you in making your decision—your values? your goals? your needs? Or your _____ with other people?

A Decision-Making Chart

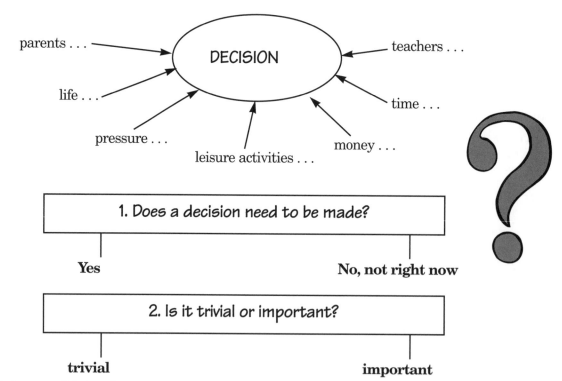

parents . . .

teachers . . .

DECISION

life . . .

time . . .

pressure . . .

money . . .

leisure activities . . .

1. Does a decision need to be made?

Yes

No, not right now

2. Is it trivial or important?

trivial

Is it reversible? Is there little risk?

important

Are many people involved in this decision?
Do the consequences affect long-range plans?
Is this an urgent decision?

3. Do you need to get more information?

What will it cost in terms of:

- time
- money
- commitment
- relationships

Is it a real possibility for you? Are other people supportive?

4. How does this decision affect you and your goals?

Right on track!

Not sure—might need to rethink goals!

5. What is the basis for your decision?

- right in line with what you really want
- consistent with your values
- not at the expense of other people

Worksheet #98   What Decision Needs to Be Made?

In each of these situations, someone needs to make a decision. Identify the decision in each. Use the questions on the chart from worksheet #97 to help someone come up with a good decision.

1. Ginger, your golden retriever, is 15 years old and can't walk anymore. She seems to be in pain.

    _____

2. Grandma is 85 and can't walk anymore. She is afraid to be left alone and is in constant pain from her arthritis.

    _____

3. It's two days until graduation. Your father wants to know what you're planning to do after that.

    _____

4. The house your family has always admired has finally come up for sale!

    _____

5. Your friend Janelle doesn't want to work or go to school. She'd like to get married and have someone take care of her all the time.

    _____

6. You just found out you got an extra week's vacation this year—plus a large bonus.

    _____

7. After skiing a double black run at a Wyoming ski resort, you encounter a tree. Your leg is starting to swell and hurts more than anything else you can remember.

    _____

8. It's late at night, you're alone, and you hear some noises outside in your front yard.

    _____

9. Everyone has gathered at your house and they're all hungry.

    _____

10. You were out late last night and didn't have time to study for your huge history final that is during the first hour this morning.

    _____

Worksheet #99

Trivial vs. Important

Which of these decisions are trivial? Which are important? What is the basis for your conclusion?

1. What color eye shadow should I use? Well . . . I'm wearing a blue dress. I guess blue would be OK.

Hurry up, dear.

_____
_____
_____

2. If we bomb that small country, we will gain respect for our strength. On the other hand, bombing a small country could make us look like bullies.

_____
_____
_____

3. This is an experimental drug. Some of the side effects are pretty nasty. But, it could save your life.

_____
_____
_____

4. If you sew this dress carefully, it will look great at your wedding.

_____
_____
_____

5. You can either do a traditional book report or try one of the creative projects instead. Your grade will be evaluated the same.

_____
_____
_____

6. Sign on the dotted line! I'll make you a movie star!!

_____
_____
_____

7. You are an excellent athlete! If you keep looking really good, I know there are some colleges that would be interested in offering you a scholarship.

_____
_____
_____

Name_____ Date _____

Worksheet #100 **When You Need More Information**

What further information might these people need to make a good decision?

1. *Wow! This car is SOOOOOO cool! I think I can make the payments . . . I love it!*

_____

_____

_____

2. *There are two flights to California. One leaves in the middle of the night, but it's really cheap. And we might have to change planes three times.*

_____

_____

_____

3. *Grandma sent you some birthday money. She wants you to buy a computer.*

_____

_____

_____

4. *My cousin Mark wants to ask you out. He goes to another school, but he's seen your picture and likes what he sees.*

_____

_____

_____

5. *You can either go out for track or play soccer. Sign-up is tonight after school.*

_____

_____

_____

6. *If you take history in the summer, you'll probably get Mr. Peters. He's really easy and you'll have an easy A. But you probably won't learn anything.*

_____

_____

_____

7. *Sure you can drive the car, son. Just find out how much the car insurance is and let me know how you plan to pay for it!*

_____

_____

_____

8. *Wow! Here's an ad for making $100 a week in cash! You can work part-time from your own home! This sounds too good to be true!*

_____

_____

_____

Name_____ Date _____

Decisions That Affect Other People

What types of decisions have these individuals made in their lives? How will it affect other people?

1. Dr. Corbin is a children's dentist. He is very patient with kids and tries very hard to make their visits fun and pain-free.

   _____

2. Mr. Smith works very hard at a factory at night. During the day he sleeps and in the evenings he has some beers with his friends. He doesn't spend a lot of time with his children.

   _____

3. Dr. Peterson is a college professor who is supposed to teach English, but he doesn't seem to spend a lot of time preparing his classes. He doesn't return the students' work quickly and gives very little feedback.

   _____

4. Karen is a nurse who works with very sick people. She is outgoing, friendly, and refuses to let any of them put her in a bad mood, even though they may be crabby and in a lot of pain.

   _____

5. Markie works at a fast-food restaurant. He is more interested in flirting with Cheri, the "french fry queen," instead of listening to the orders given through the drive-up window.

   _____

6. Jan is a florist who puts forth a lot of extra effort to make sure that the weddings she works on are just perfect. The flower arrangements are beautiful, she is always sure to be at the church early, and she adds a lot of her own creative ideas.

   _____

7. Mr. Benchley is a salesman for house siding who is always late to his appointments.

   _____

8. Bob Woodman is a building contractor who uses the cheapest materials available to build houses.

   _____

9. Coach Davis encourages her players to do their best and spends extra time helping them with their weak areas. Many players don't want to play for her, though, because her rules are even stricter than the school's rules.

   _____

10. Flash is a hot-shot basketball player who usually scores the most points for the team, but he doesn't like to pass the ball to anyone else.

   _____

Name_____ Date _____

Head vs. Heart Decisions

Sometimes decisions are made impulsively—with the heart, not the head. Intuition is not always a bad thing, but don't throw common sense out the window. These decisions were made impulsively. Do you think the outcomes are OK? Why or why not?

1. I think we should buy 1000 shares of this new software company. I have studied a lot about computers. I have a good feeling about this.

_____
_____
_____

2. John is sensible, secure, and has a good job—but Ralph is exciting and carefree. He is so much fun to be with. I guess I'll marry Ralph. My parents will just die!

_____
_____
_____

3. Oh, what a cute puppy!! He'll be so big, but our apartment is small right now. I know it says NO PETS, but we can keep him hidden. We'll teach him not to bark.

_____
_____

4. My entire paycheck is spent. But I really want that new stereo. I can buy it on time payments.

_____
_____

5. I know I'd make more money by being a doctor like my dad, but I think I'd be happier teaching kindergarten kids. I love kids.

_____
_____
_____

6. I've got two extra tickets to the game. I know they're sold out and I could sell them . . . but why don't you just take them and ask a friend to go with you? Sometime you can do me a favor!

_____
_____

Skill 19—Viewing Situations Realistically

INSTRUCTOR PAGE

Rationale: We all have visions of grandeur—someday life will be wonderful, we'll have those bills paid off, people will adore us, etc., etc. But, life is a school of hard knocks and we must learn to put ourselves into situations realistically. This includes the ability to see ourselves as we are, to know what needs to be changed to better our situations, and then to go ahead and make those changes.

WORKSHEETS

Worksheet #103: Making Realistic Changes

This worksheet contains comments about how hard it is to realistically assess ourselves. Others may not want to be honest with us or be able to make accurate assessments. We may not want to hear what they have to say, anyway. Students are to begin thinking about why change is necessary and how important it is to be open and realistic about making changes.

Answer Key:

1. situation, abilities; 2. honest, able; 3. look, situation; 4. changes; 5. positive, possible; 6. attitude

Worksheet #104: Improbable or Impossible?

Students are to read the scenarios of the characters and decide how possible or probable the outcomes will be.

Answer Key: (answers may vary)

1. possible—if he's a good listener

2. improbable—he seems very confident but has a lot of hurdles to get over

3. improbable—if she doesn't like math or science, she'll probably have trouble learning about helicopter repair

4. possible—she may be a really good guitarist and songwriter, but improbable that she'll make millions at it

5. improbable—this boy doesn't sound like he really wants to work at all

6. possible—depending on how well she's taught her parents to cater to her

7. improbable—26 miles is a lot longer than running around the block; however, it could be possible if he began training

8. possible—if she's lucky and a good writer; but more likely improbable—it's hard to get something published!

Worksheet #105: Making Changes for the Better: Habits and Friends

Students are to decide whether the characters on the worksheet need to make changes in their habits or in their friends.

Answer Key:

1. habits; 2. habits; 3. friends; 4. friends; 5. habits; 6. friends

Worksheet #106: Making Changes for the Better: Attitudes and Actions

Students are to decide whether the characters on the worksheet need to make changes in their attitudes or actions.

Answer Key:

1. attitude (toward learning)

2. actions

3. attitude (toward following rules) or actions (actually following the rules)

4. attitude (toward cleaning the room)

5. actions (sitting with Art)

6. attitude (the boy is the spoiled one!)

Worksheet #107: It Could Happen . . .

Sometimes what is annoying or a distraction when you are younger may grow into a strength, a job, or an attraction when you are older! Students are to evaluate how seemingly trivial skills might grow into something important. Then they can have fun with developing their own examples.

Answer Key:

1. likes to sew—becomes a surgeon

2. wants attention—becomes a comedian

3. likes to talk—becomes a radio disc jockey

4. likes to draw—becomes an artist

5. is good with computers—owns computer stores

6. likes to argue—becomes a lawyer

7. loves animals—becomes a vet

TEACHER TIPS

- Be realistic with your students about their assignments, comments, abilities, performance on projects, etc., but try to be positive whenever possible. Emphasize the social skills they have learned and used.

- Spend time with individual students to go over their academic skills. You are the authority and great evaluator in this area. Help them understand their learning strengths and weaknesses. Give suggestions for strengthening academic areas.

- Some schools offer informal vocational interest tests. Have students begin thinking about their strengths and interests. Help them make some small steps towards making their dreams possible. Suggest volunteer work in areas of their interest, point out job opportunities, have guest speakers drop by to talk about interests, and don't forget the school counselor who may be able to lend insight into the job market.

- Some students may be in a situation in which their home lives are destructive (abusive, neglectful, ignored, etc.) and it is frustrating to think that the student is helpless and sees hopelessness as his or her only future. Keep reinforcing that change is possible and that there are resources available. Time changes things. Let them know you are there for them.

PARENT POINTERS

- Try to keep lines of communication open between you and your child by discussing what he or she is interested in, what he or she wishes were different about life, and how the future appears. You don't need to go into specifics, but a general conversation will reveal his or her feelings about the future.

- Give your child as many opportunities as possible to explore different interests and develop strengths. This will affirm his or her talents and give you something positive to experience together. There are social skills to be learned by going white-water rafting with a school group, doing volunteer work at a soup kitchen, and trailing you around for a day on your job.

- Comment positively when you observe your child making changes for the better. ("I appreciate you doing the laundry last night when we were all so busy—you saw what needed to be done and did it. Thank you.")

- Make a positive change commitment to do something in front of your child—then do it! Start exercising! Quit smoking! Use better, richer vocabulary words! Turn off the soaps and watch the news! You are a powerful model!

- Not every child needs to set a goal to make a lot of money, become famous, go to Harvard, get a football scholarship, or marry a millionaire. Most of us are just plain people with ordinary lives. But we all have dreams. Some people take a little longer to figure out what they really want or need to do with their lives. Unless your child is in danger or in urgent need of a decision, try to give him or her as much time as possible to figure things out and to make things happen.

- Parents with a lot of resources (money, influence, etc.) might want to do a lot to make sure their child is equally successful—however that is defined. Realize that your child must learn to be independent and that the things gained by being resourceful and independent are worth a lot. Hold back sometimes in order to teach a lesson.

PRACTICE ACTIVITIES

. . . Continue using the journal as a means for students to collect and express their thoughts. Some entry ideas might include:

- My Personal Inventory
- What I Hear Others Say About Me
- Changes I Wish I Could Make in My Life
- 20 Years from Now . . .
- How I Wish My Future Would Be

. . . Invite successful speakers to come to your class to give brief autobiographies of how they ended up where they did. What changes did they have to make in their lives to reach their goals? What sacrifices? What risks? What would they change as they look back on their youth?

. . . If appropriate, invite a social worker to speak to your class or someone who has either had a rough past or worked with people who have had to overcome a lot to "make it." Many students don't realize how many people have had major changes to overcome.

. . . Have students anonymously write positive (positive only!) comments about each other in a special book or circulated sheet. Students can sometimes be quite perceptive and truthful. As long as this is kept as a self-esteem-building activity, it may help students see how others view them and what strengths they may be overlooking.

Name_____ Date _____

Making Realistic Changes

Being realistic about yourself, your situation, and your abilities is a tough skill to conquer. Then add the ability to be bold enough to make needed changes in the above areas and you have a real challenge!

If you listen to what other people say about you, you might be happy—especially if you enjoy hearing your mother brag about how cute you are and what a genius you have turned out to be (all from her side of the family, of course). But if you hear your dad constantly nag you about how lazy you are and that you'll probably never amount to anything—you could have an entirely different impression of yourself. Are either of these realistic? Does it matter what others say about you?

Your mother and father may not be 100% objective about your good and bad points. But do you really want to hear your best friend tell you that you're overweight, have pimples, and need to use more deodorant? Do you want your teacher to constantly remind you of your lack of creativity and initiative? There are some things none of us really want to hear or know about ourselves!

Some people may not want to be completely honest with you—or may not be able to be honest with you—about your realistic abilities. You have to take a look at yourself and give yourself and your situation some serious thought.

But sometimes it really is better to recognize that we need to make changes—in ourselves, our situations, and our attitudes. It may help to take an honest inventory of your present situation (good or bad) and think about what changes are positive and possible!

And don't forget—your attitude colors how you see everything. A good attitude can take care of many bad situations.

1. It is important to be realistic about yourself, your _____ , and your _____ .

2. Some people may not want to be completely _____ with you about yourself or may not be _____ to realistically tell you about yourself.

3. You have to take a _____ at yourself and give some serious thought to yourself and your _____ .

4. It might be in your best interest to make some _____ in your life.

5. Changes need to be _____ and _____ .

6. Remember, too, that your _____ affects how you see things.

Name_____ Date _____

Improbable or Impossible?

These characters all have dreams for the future. Do you think they are IMPROBABLE—probably not likely to happen; or IMPOSSIBLE—will not happen? Why?

1. I know there's a test tomorrow on Chapter 16 and I haven't done any of the assignments, but I'm a good listener and I know I'll at least pass the test.

_____
_____
_____

2. I'm going to ask the most popular girl in school to go to the prom with me. It doesn't bother me that she's going steady with the class president. With my looks and charm, she'll say yes.

_____
_____
_____

3. I can't wait to fly and repair helicopters in the Army. Then I can quit high school and quit taking these stupid math and science classes.

_____
_____
_____

4. I know I'm a good guitarist and song writer—I'm planning to go on tour and make millions!  TWANG!!!

_____
_____
_____

5. Yes, I want the job, but not if I have to do something I really don't like. No one's telling me what to do, especially rude customers. And I'm not working any mornings.

_____
_____
_____

6. I don't need to worry about a job—mommy and daddy will always take care of their little princess!

_____
_____
_____

7. Hey, let's run the New York Marathon! Wouldn't that be fun? I ran around the block once without stopping!

_____
_____
_____

8. I'm going to write a novel. A mystery. A best-seller! How hard can it be? I got a C+ on my creative writing story!

_____
_____
_____

Name_____ Date _____

Making Changes for the Better:
Habits and Friends

Which of these characters need to make changes in their habits? Which need to make changes in their friends?

1. *Every Friday we all go bowling and then drink beer until we're sick. Can't we try something new and different?*

_____
_____
_____

2. *I'm up to five packs a day. This is getting out of hand.*

_____
_____
_____

3. *So we're in a little trouble with the police. We won't get caught. Come on, we have a big deal going on this weekend. We'll be OK.*

_____
_____
_____

4. *Who should we talk about today? Terri? She's such a flirt. I can't stand her.*

I can't either.

I'm so tired of all the gossip. I wonder what they say about me?

_____
_____

5. *How did I gain 15 pounds? Where did this come from??? Maybe I should start . . . exercising!!??*

_____
_____

6. *Can I borrow some money, Bud?*

I need to use your car this weekend. I knew YOU wouldn't mind.

Well, could you put some gas in it this time?

_____
_____
_____

Name_____ Date _____

Making Changes for the Better:
Attitudes and Actions

Sometimes a change in attitude or a change in action or behavior can make a situation better. Which might be helpful for these characters?

1. I'm assigning three extra reports this month. I think the extra work will prepare you for your writing exam at the end of the semester.

Oh no! I don't want any more work! I don't want to learn anything else.

_____
_____

2. Wow! I dropped from B's to C's in every class! I think I should start studying more. And unplug the TV, radio, computer, and . . . probably my hair dryer, too.

_____
_____

3. You are getting home late every night, young man! We have set a curfew for you, you know. You're not following it, so how can you expect us to give you the car when we don't even trust you to follow our basic rules?

I need to follow the rules. I'm not doing anything wrong, but I have to have my parents' trust.

_____
_____

4. We're having company this week-end. Please clean up your room before you go out.

My room is my property. I can just close the door.

_____
_____

5. Everybody is so mean to Art. I know he's a little odd, but really—they are so cruel.

Maybe I will.

Why don't you sit with him at lunch?

_____
_____

6. Sorry, Charlie, your dad didn't get the extra week's vacation like we thought. Dad has to work.

Everybody is just out to ruin my fun!! My whole summer is spoiled!

_____
_____

Name_____ Date _____

It Could Happen . . .

Don't overlook your talents and things you like to do. Even though it may not seem realistic right now, you might end up doing something you really like to do! How might these characters have happy endings?

1. Martha loves to sew!

2. Jack is the class clown.

3. Estelle is a motor-mouth; she won't quit talking.

4. Barney doodles all over his papers, desk, arm, and even walls!

5. Fred is a computer whiz.

6. Joy argues about everything.

7. Sara loves animals.

Add your own . . .

_____

_____

_____

_____

Skill 20—Being Flexible

INSTRUCTOR PAGE

Rationale: Things can't always go our way. We can either accept it and go on, or fight it and possibly lose, or not think about it and have no opinion at all. But some things are worth thinking about and forming an opinion about, even if that opinion changes over time as we have more information, more experiences, and more opportunity to understand situations. Being flexible is more than letting others run all over you; it is making a conscious effort to handle something in a different way without getting upset.

WORKSHEETS

Worksheet #108: Handling Changes

Students are to read the paragraphs about why changes are uncomfortable, yet sometimes helpful.

Answer Key:

1. safe; 2. natural; 3. adapt, stronger; 4. surprises; 5. stronger, think; 6. attitude

Worksheet #109: Changing Your Plans

Sometimes plans don't go your way. Students are to think about what they might do in situations in which they have had plans interrupted.

Answer Key: (answers may vary)

1. go with your friends to the Chinese restaurant and look for something on the menu that looks familiar

2. spend free time at your friend's house, watching his TV

3. do your best on your chapter and don't be late again

4. have someone tape the show for you while you're at work

5. let them finish their game if they'll stop after one game

6. drop off your sister and friends at the movie, have them get a ride home with someone else

Worksheet #110: Changing Your Mind

Sometimes people change their minds because they have more information, have a new experience, or bow to pressure from others. Students are to suggest what might have occurred to change the minds of the characters on the worksheets.

Answer Key: (answers may vary)

1. she never tried mushrooms before

2. he has spent a lot of time on airplanes without any accidents

3. he only wants to back a winner

4. the cost of the shoes is not worth what she wants to pay for them

5. the boy has learned that the author has only one basic plot

6. the girl never spends time with Jessie; after doing so, she realized that Jessie was fun

7. the boy was probably repeating someone else's opinion

8. the girl didn't read the directions

Worksheet #111: Being Open to New Things

Students are to think about ways that they can be flexible by being open to new things, or having an open attitude about new things. A suggestion is given for each on the worksheet; students are to think of their own examples.

Answers will vary.

Worksheet #112: Reflecting

Many people don't take the time to truly reflect or think about situations. Reflecting about something may give you time to form an opinion or change an opinion. Students are to select which of the examples demonstrate (a) reaffirming an existing position or belief, (b) being open to the possibility that you might change your mind, or (c) completely changing your mind.

Answer Key:

1. b—he is considering other opinions and ideas
2. c—her opinion completely changed about her teacher
3. a—he believes in honesty

TEACHER TIPS

- When a change of plans becomes necessary in the course of your day, ask your students to suggest alternatives to handle the situation. Brainstorm some possibilities; then select one to try out.

- Be a good model of "rolling with the punches" when your plans go awry. Instead of having the attitude, "Oh no, here's another ruined plan!" demonstrate the attitude of "Well, here's an opportunity to be creative!"

- Always have a back-up plan or a menu of activities to fall back on. This is good for days when there is an unexpected substitute in your room.

PARENT POINTERS

- When appropriate, explain to your child how and why unexpected events came about—a surprise visit, a spent paycheck, an unexpected car repair, etc. Use this as an opportunity to show him or her how cause-and-effect works.

- Explain the difference between being flexible and bending rules too far. Socially, it may be necessary to give in a little (company coming over, later curfew for a party, etc.), but insist on enforcing the absolutes—whatever they may be for your family and child (no drugs, no driving after drinking, etc.).

PRACTICE ACTIVITIES

. . . Arrange to have students work on a unit in which they are given a lot of flexibility as to how they complete the task(s) involved. This might include doing two reports for a B, two reports plus a demonstration for an A, etc. But give students the opportunity to map out their plan and to use resources and time to reach their goal. Sharing materials will probably require students to be flexible about when and what they do.

. . . Use cooperative groups occasionally to encourage students to be flexible about their roles. Arrange groups so that each student has a chance to be the leader, secretary/recorder, speaker/summarizer, etc., for the group. If students complain about their role, remind them that flexibility in this case involves changing roles from time to time.

. . . Before assigning a taxing or challenging assignment, prepare those students who will be distraught and/or fall apart without guidance to follow. These students may need to devise a Plan B to help themselves accomplish the work. ("In the event that the book you need for your book report is out, what might you do instead?" Select another book/find out when the book is due back/select a new topic for which there are lots of books, etc.)

Name_____   Date _____

Handling Changes

There is something safe about predictability—knowing that dinner will be at 6, the final spelling test will always be on Friday, that you'll work at the Burger Hut every summer for the rest of your life, or that your best friend will always be there for you.

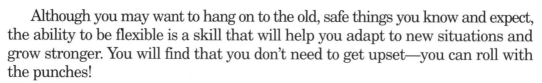

However, changes are inevitable and natural. And, they can be good for you. When Mom gets a new job, supper may be whenever you make it. The spelling test may be postponed to Monday if there's a special program. Burger Hut may go out of business and close. Your best friend may move to Iowa.

Although you may want to hang on to the old, safe things you know and expect, the ability to be flexible is a skill that will help you adapt to new situations and grow stronger. You will find that you don't need to get upset—you can roll with the punches!

Change can be good. It can make you stronger. It can make you think. It can prepare you to handle the surprises that life will throw at you. Life is full of them!

Decide that your attitude will be positive about changes. Some things you can control and change. Do it! Other things you have no control over—you might get sick or move or have to react to someone else's decisions. Decide that you'll handle it. You'll make a new plan, find something positive about it, and go on. You will!!

1. Predictable things can make us feel _____ .

2. Changes are inevitable and _____ .

3. The ability to be flexible can help you _____ to new situations and help you grow _____ .

4. You shouldn't be surprised that life is full of _____ .

5. Change can be good because it can make you _____ and make you _____ .

6. Decide that your _____ will be positive about changes.

Name_____ Date _____

Changing Your Plans

How could you be flexible in the following situations?

1. Everyone wants to go out for Chinese food but you. You suggest a place that serves hamburgers and fries (greasy, but cheap), but no one seems interested. What will you do?

2. Guess what? Aunt Vivian and her three cats are coming for a week-long visit and Mom has graciously offered them your room—which places you in the basement, away from your computer, stereo, and TV. What will you do?

3. Your friends have formed a study group to help each other pass biology. Everyone has a different chapter to review and share notes with the group. You were late to the study group and dismayed to find out that they saved the longest, hardest, and most boring chapter for you to do! What will you do?

4. You have watched The Three Stooges every night at 10 P.M. for as long as you can remember. But now, with your new job, you're expected to work evenings. The money is nice, but . . . What will you do?

5. You signed up for the city tennis court #3 for one hour—from 6 to 7 P.M. But lo and behold! Some other people are on your court at 6:10! You explained that you were late, but it was still your time to play. They insisted that they waited, but no one showed up so they assumed they could have it. Their game has already started and they want to finish. What will you do?

6. Your sister wants to borrow the family car to go to a movie with her friends. You already told your friends that you'd have a car to go to a party—also Friday night. Your mom's advice: "Work it out." What will you do?

Name_____ Date _____

Changing Your Mind

What happened to cause these characters to change their minds?

1.

I hate mushrooms! I will never eat anything with a mushroom on it!

Sure—mushroom soup.

Hey—this soup is really good! Can you give me the recipe?

I guess I do like mushrooms!

_____

_____

2.

200 flights later . . .

Flying is dangerous. I just know we're going to fall out of the sky!

Well, do we get a movie on this flight? I'm so glad I can relax and read a book. I love to look out the window and see the clouds.

_____

_____

3.

Go Pacers! That's my team!

They're behind by 20 points.

Go Bulls! Yeaa—all the way! That's my team!

_____

_____

4.

These shoes are perfect! They are exactly what I want!

That'll be $185.

I think I'll keep looking.

_____

_____

5.

Hey, this book is great! This author is so creative!

5 books later . . .

It's the same story over and over. I'm on Chapter One and I can already tell you who murdered the guy.

_____

_____

6.

I would never invite Jessie to a party! She's so dull and just talks about herself all the time. Bor—ing!

I think she's just shy. Have you ever tried to get to know her? She's really fun.

Wow, we have a lot in common. I didn't realize she likes to play basketball, too! Let's run together.

_____

_____

7.

Don't ever buy an American car. They are all junk.

Here, son—keys to your first car! American-made, of course!

Of course! It's my dream car! I love it! God bless America!

_____

_____

8.

I can't figure out why my bread turns out so flat. I guess the breadmaker is broken.

Here, read the directions. You forgot to add all of the ingredients. Like yeast.

I love homemade bread! It's so easy to make!!

_____

_____

Name_____ Date _____

Being Open to New Things

What are some ways you can LEARN something new?

I'm sorry. I will never understand how to operate a computer! It's beyond me!

_____
_____
_____
_____
_____

. . . TRY something new?

White-water rafting? Me? Well . . . if it's safe . . . why not! I'll go!

_____
_____
_____
_____
_____

. . . become more INFORMED?

Oh, come on, let's watch cartoons!

CNN reports that . . .

_____
_____
_____
_____
_____

. . . EXPAND your skills?

I know you like to cook. Would you be interested in joining me in a French cooking class at the Y?

_____
_____
_____
_____
_____

. . . LISTEN to a different opinion?

Please don't make up your mind about who to vote for until you've heard what my candidate has to say!

_____
_____
_____
_____
_____

Name_____ Date _____

Reflecting

Sometimes we are quick to give an opinion—or always feel we are right. The process of reflecting on something, taking time to think about it, can lead you to:

a. reaffirm that you ARE right;

b. open up the possibility that you could be wrong or might want to change your mind;

c. allow for the possibility that you now believe something different and are mature enough to change your mind.

Which of these scenarios illustrates **a**, **b**, or **c**?

_____ 1.

I've always believed that abortion is OK under some circumstances. But now that my sister is unhappily pregnant, it all seems different. I find myself imagining what the baby will look like—and become! I know that my sister is unhappy and there are many negative sides to this—but I'm starting to read about how unborn babies can feel pain and have heartbeats. Now I'm not sure anymore that I agree with abortion in all circumstances.

_____ 2.

Mrs. Brown was the toughest high school reading teacher I ever had! She gave us so much work and reading to do—I thought I could never keep up! I HATED her! She made us correct every single mistake and rewrite every paragraph until it was perfect. I could never figure out why it mattered to her so much. Now that I'm in college, though, Freshman Composition is a breeze! I complained so much in high school, but now I have so many skills I can breeze through all this stuff and I'm way ahead of most of the rest of my class! Thank you, Mrs. Brown!

_____ 3.

I always felt uncomfortable when my friends would steal things—like books from the library, tips from a restaurant table, and even shoplifting just for fun. But I would never do it. It just seemed to me that it's wrong, even if nobody catches you. I'm proud that I'm honest—and I work for what I have. I don't get my thrills by cheating others. I will always be this way. I am an honest person. You can ask anybody!

Part II

Social Skills
in Action

Social Skills Applied at Home
Routine Situations

INSTRUCTOR PAGE

Introduction: This series of worksheets allows the learner to practice identifying specific social skills that may be helpful in dealing with routine, or common, situations encountered in the home environment.

WORKSHEETS

Note: Answers to the worksheets will vary according to the ages and developmental stages of your students. The answers provided in the Answer Keys are models for typical responses you should expect from your students. As with any other activity, accept answers that can be logically supported by facts.

Worksheet #1: Getting Along With Parents

Answer Key:

1. C; 2. A; 3. B

Worksheet #2: Getting Along With Siblings

Answer Key:

1. B; 2. C; 3. A

Worksheet #3: Balancing Responsibilities and Desires

Answer Key:

1. buying a car vs. waiting to buy; using common sense
2. doing chores vs. going with friends; being flexible
3. getting a puppy vs. no puppy; assessing a situation
4. help with sale vs. babysit; negotiating or compromising

Worksheet #4: Helping to Maintain a Supportive Family Environment

Answer Key:

1. C, D; 2. A; 3. B

Worksheet #5: Giving and Taking Within the Family

Answer Key:

1. work out a schedule for sharing the car
2. really pay attention to the instruction given
3. discuss with parent when unexpected guests may arrive
4. handle the problem calmly; put energy into finding something else to eat
5. the parent will probably trust the child if he or she uses the phone at the party
6. the parent might avoid pressuring his son to go out for baseball
7. sharing the financial status might encourage everyone to be more thrifty
8. sharing a job lightens the load for everyone

Name_____   Date _____

Getting Along with Parents

Which of the following social skills might be involved in getting along with parents on a day-to-day basis?

A. Being a Good Listener, B. Using Humor Appropriately, C. Understanding Another's Point of View

---

1.

2.

3.

Name_____ Date _____

Getting Along with Siblings

Which social skills could you use to respond to these situations with siblings?
A. Negotiating or Compromising, B. Controlling Emotions, C. Reading Other's Moods

1.

2.

3.

Name_____ Date _____

Balancing Responsibilities and Desires

Each of the characters below has a conflict between something that should be done and something that he or she would like to do. First, identify the conflict in each situation. Then, identify some social skills that would help resolve the situations.

Examples: Assessing a Situation

               Using Common Sense

Situation #1

Fred wants to buy a car. He doesn't have a lot of money and can't afford one right now, but he doesn't have a lot of time, either, to hold down a job to make money to buy the car.

Conflict: _____

Social Skill: _____

Situation #2

One of Carl's chores around the house is to keep the lawn neatly mowed every week. He doesn't mind mowing, but this weekend is beautiful and his friends are getting a group together to go to the beach for a cookout and volleyball. It's Saturday morning and the group is leaving in about an hour.

Conflict: _____

Social Skill: _____

Situation #3

Alison's friend's dog just had puppies—eight beautiful, little, black, wiggly babies. Alison didn't think her mother would mind if she told the friend that they could probably take two or three of them. After all, Alison intends to do all of the work involved in caring for them.

Conflict: _____

Social Skill: _____

Situation #4

Martha's family is having a garage sale this weekend. Martha promised to help organize everything and stick around to help collect all of the money that will come pouring in! At the last minute, a neighbor called to ask if she could babysit—it's not really an emergency, but she REALLY needs to do some errands.

Conflict: _____

Social Skill: _____

Helping to Maintain a Supportive Family Environment

Match the social skill that is involved in the following examples of family members being supportive of each other.

A—Being Able to Communicate
B—Reading Others' Moods, etc.
C—Revealing Yourself to Others
D—Using Humor

Name_____ Date _____

Giving and Taking within the Family

How could the following social skills help this family give-and-take in the situations to help work out the problems?

1. Being Flexible

I need to use the car sometime this week. When would be a good time?

_____

_____

2. Good Listener

Will you help me with my math? I don't understand prime numbers!

_____

_____

3. Another's Point of View

Please don't bring people over without giving me notice. It embarrasses me when the house is a mess!

_____

_____

4. Controlling Emotions

There's no cereal!! What am I supposed to eat for breakfast? Doesn't anyone ever go shopping around here!? I'm MAD! And I'm HUNGRY!!

_____

_____

5. Negotiating

I'll give you the car phone, but I expect you to call me when you are leaving the party. Then I won't worry about you being late.

_____

_____

6. Revealing Self

You'll probably be disappointed, Dad, but I don't want to go out for baseball. I really don't even like to play that much.

_____

_____

7. Assessing Situation

Money is tight this month, kids. Do we really need to go shopping for new athletic shoes?

_____

_____

8. Working with Others

We're painting the basement this weekend! I've got brushes and lots of energy! It'll be FUN!!!!!

_____

_____

Social Skills Applied at Home
Problems or Unusual Situations

INSTRUCTOR PAGE

Introduction: Every family encounters problems or unusual situations to resolve. In this section, there is opportunity for applying specific social skills to problematic situations regarding the home.

WORKSHEETS

Note: Answers to the worksheets will vary according to the ages and developmental stages of your students. The answers provided in the Answer Keys are models for typical responses you should expect from your students. As with any other activity, accept answers that can be logically supported by facts.

Worksheet #6: Handling a Divorce or Family Split

Answer Key:

1. understanding another's point of view; 2. assessing a situation; 3. understanding another's point of view; 4. assessing a situation; 5. controlling emotions; 6. being flexible

Worksheet #7: Intrusions on Privacy

Answer Key:

1. talk about why privacy is important

2. agree to let people in your room by invitation

3. put up a sign that humorously states your feelings

4. realize that sometimes you may have to share your space

Worksheet #8: Changing Roles and Demands

Answer Key:

1. being able to negotiate; 2. working with others; 3. reacting appropriately to peer pressure; 4. viewing yourself realistically; 5. making a good impression; 6. being flexible

Worksheet #9: Dealing With Poor Self-Esteem

Answer Key:

1. making a good impression

2. revealing yourself to others

3. making healthy decisions

4. common sense

5. being able to communicate

Worksheet #10: Living With Abusive or Dysfunctional Family Members

Answer Key:

1. don't be too judgmental

2. find out facts and information on the problem

3. share your concerns

4. seek out help

5. decide to make decisions that will be healthy, not add to a harmful situation

Worksheet #6   # Handling a Divorce or Family Split

What social skills might be helpful in these situations?

1.

> I don't want Dad to leave. Can't you just stay together?

_____
_____
_____
_____

2.

> I'm moving in with Mom. She's a lot easier to deal with!

_____
_____
_____
_____

3.

> I'm going to have to go back to work. Everything will be different for us.

_____
_____
_____

4.

> Stepbrother? What's all this about a stepbrother? I LIKE being an only child!

_____
_____
_____

5.

> WHAT? Mom's going to get married again? No way!!

_____
_____
_____

6.

> Half a year with Mom, half a year with Dad. I hate it. I don't think it's fair.

_____
_____
_____

Name_____ Date _____

Intrusions on Privacy

How could these social skills help someone handle having his or her privacy taken away or
intruded on?

Being Able to Communicate

_____

_____

_____

_____

_____

_____

Negotiating or Compromising

_____

_____

_____

_____

_____

Using Humor

_____

_____

_____

_____

Being Flexible

_____

_____

_____

_____

_____

Name_____   Date _____

Changing Roles and Demands

What are some roles or demands that might change during someone's lifetime? What social skills could help? Add to this list:

1. having a new sister or brother

2. getting a part-time job

3. going from junior high or middle school to high school

4. finding out that you have leukemia

5. moving to a new state

6. taking a hard class in school

_____

_____

_____

_____

_____

_____

_____

_____

_____

_____

Name_____ Date _____

Dealing with Poor Self-Esteem

These characters are making comments that sound as though they reflect low self-esteem. What social skills would you recommend that each person work on?

1.

I don't have any friends—no one likes me.

_____
_____
_____
_____

2.

Why does everyone think I'm stuck up?

_____
_____
_____
_____

3.

I guess I should dress up for the job interview, but I probably won't get it anyway, so why bother?

_____
_____
_____
_____

4.

If I get a good grade on my project, the teacher might make me stand up and tell about it. I don't really care what I get.

_____
_____
_____

5.

Why would Jeff be interested in talking to me? I just won't say anything to him when he goes by.

_____
_____
_____
_____

Name_____   Date _____

Living with Abusive or Dysfunctional Family Members

Some people in your home may have problems that are beyond your control. Examples of problems:

alcoholism

depression

extremely bad temper

unable to work, disabled

How could these social skills help?

Looks like Dad's really out of it. This is not a good time to ask for help with my algebra!

1. Understanding Another's Point of View

_____

_____

_____

2. Being Able to Assess a Situation

_____

_____

_____

3. Revealing Yourself to Others

_____

_____

_____

4. Initiating Positive Contact

_____

_____

_____

5. Making Healthy Decisions in Social Situations

_____

_____

_____

Social Skills Applied at Home
Enhancing the Family or Home Situation

INSTRUCTOR PAGE

Introduction: A close family can make the home environment a truly delightful place to be. Social skills that encourage sharing, support for each other, and self-disclosure can bring a family closer together.

WORKSHEETS

Note: Answers to the worksheets will vary according to the age and developmental stages of your students. The answers provided in the Answer Keys are models for typical responses you should expect from your students. As with any other activity, accept answers that can be logically supported by facts.

Worksheet #11: Spending Quality Time Together

Answer Key:

1. encouraging each other; understanding another's point of view
2. sharing chores; working with others
3. playing games together; reading others' moods
4. listening; being a good listener
5. handling time problems; negotiating

Worksheet #12: Setting Family Goals

Answer Key:

1. family having a chat about their daily activities
2. go for a walk each evening
3. talk about social problem depicted on TV show
4. use opportunities that arise at work to elicit discussion about pressure
5. when making plans, build in a back-up plan

Worksheet #13: Strengthening Each Other

Answer Key:

1. "Would you like me to help you study?"
2. be more available to her
3. "You probably won't—you're a terrific player!"
4. listen to her practice her speech
5. "Would you like to talk about it?"
6. help share the chores to allow her to get some sleep

Worksheet #14: Learning About One's Family

Answer Key:

1. listen to old stories
2. talk to relatives about family events
3. develop friendships

4. maintain a relationship

5. be a good listener

6. find out about distant relatives (anyone famous?)

7. assess situations

Worksheet #15: Going Beyond What Is Expected of Each Other

Answer Key:

1. clean out the basement also

2. prepare dinner and clean up the kitchen

3. get A's

4. do the chores without being asked

5. help anyone who needs help or share extra space in suitcase

6. help mom do the laundry

7. make the bed, put clean sheets on, pick up anything on the floor

8. do a more thorough job of cleaning

Worksheet #11 **Spending Quality Time Together**

How are these families spending quality time together? Which social skills are they using?

1.

   Go, Kara! Run!! You can do it!

   Hang in there, Sis!! Go, go, go!!

   _____
   _____
   _____
   _____

2. *I know you don't like to cook, Mom, so we're going to help you! We'll even clean up the kitchen!*

   You're so thoughtful!

   _____
   _____
   _____
   _____

3. *We've all had a hard week—let's have some fun.*

   Okay, it's Tova and I against you and Mom. Flip to see who goes first!

   _____
   _____
   _____
   _____

4. *I'm really disturbed about something one of my friends is doing. Can we talk about it over dinner?*

   Sure, let's do that.

   _____
   _____
   _____
   _____

5. *Kids, I have to work late every night this week, but let's all agree to save Saturday to go to the movies together.*

   Yeah!

   Deal!!

   _____
   _____
   _____

Name_____ Date _____

Setting Family Goals

How does each social skill below help the family achieve its goal in the situations?

1. Being a Good Listener

Family Goal: to take time daily to listen to each member of the family talk about his or her day

_____

_____

_____

2. Revealing Yourself to Others

Family Goal: to offer the opportunity daily for each member of the family to reveal things about him- or herself through conversation, comments, and actions

_____

_____

3. Standing Up for Your Beliefs

Family Goal: to discuss values, convictions, religious beliefs, etc., that the family adheres to or is investigating

_____

_____

4. Reacting Appropriately to Peer Pressure

Family Goal: to discuss how pressure affects each member of the family (on the job, in school, in social situations) and ways to respond to that pressure

_____

_____

5. Being Flexible

Family Goal: to work on "Plan B" (and each family member's responsibilities) when it is likely that an original goal or plan may not work out

_____

_____

Worksheet #13   # Strengthening Each Other

Write a comment or describe an action that would demonstrate how another family member could say or do something to strengthen another.

1. I think I'm going to fail this social studies test tomorrow.

_____
_____
_____
_____
_____

2. I'm really worried about Jenny. It seems like she won't talk to us anymore.

_____
_____
_____
_____
_____

3. What if I drop the ball? Will everyone laugh at me?

_____
_____
_____
_____

4. I get so nervous when I have to talk in front of the class. But half of the grade is based on this speech!

_____
_____
_____
_____

5. I'm having a bad day.

_____
_____
_____
_____

6. I'm so tired I can hardly think straight. How am I going to get everything done?

_____
_____
_____
_____

Learning About One's Family

What are some ways (or places or situations) in which someone can learn more about his or her family? How do these social skills come into play?

Being a Good Listener

Being Able to Assess a Situation

Maintaining Friendships

1. old journals or diaries from your grandparent's attic

2. attending a funeral

3. visiting relatives

4. writing to a cousin

5. attending a family reunion

6. tracing your family tree

7. going through old photo albums

8. _____

9. _____

10. _____

11. _____

12. _____

13. _____

14. _____

Name_____ Date _____

Going Beyond What Is
Expected of Each Other

Explain how each member of a family below could go beyond the minimum expectation for him or her in each situation.

Going Beyond

1. Bob's dad asks him to clean out the garage. _____

   _____

2. Kaneesha is babysitting for her younger sisters while her mother is working late. _____

   _____

3. Sarah's parents expect her to get at least straight B's on her report card. _____

   _____

4. David's chores include cleaning out the cat's litter box, walking the dog, and feeding the hamster. _____

   _____

5. The Miller family is planning a two-week driving vacation to the ocean. Everyone is supposed to pack his or her own suitcase. _____

   _____

6. The vacation is now over—there's a lot of dirty clothes to deal with. Mom usually gets that job. _____

   _____

7. Carla is supposed to make her bed once in a while. _____

   _____

8. Company is coming over soon, so Rich throws the dirty dishes into the sink and sweeps the kitchen dirt under the rug. _____

   _____

Social Skills Applied at Home
Routine Situations

INSTRUCTOR PAGE

Introduction: Students run into school situations on a daily basis in which social skills can and should be applied. These worksheets offer examples for students to consider, discuss, and analyze how social skills are relevant.

WORKSHEETS

Note: Answers to the worksheets will vary according to the ages and developmental stages of your students. The answers provided in the Answer Keys are models for typical responses you should expect from your students. As with any other activity, accept answers that can be logically supported by facts.

Worksheet #16: Getting Along With Teachers or Authority Figures

Answer Key:

1. being a good listener
2. reacting appropriately to peer pressure
3. being able to communicate
4. being able to assess a situation
5. reading others' moods
6. making healthy decisions
7. controlling emotions
8. making a good impression
9. developing a good reputation
10. standing up for your beliefs

Worksheet #17: Getting Along With Peers

Answer Key:

1. having a food fight
2. playing team sports
3. cheering
4. walking with friends
5. sitting with friends
6. being noticed
7. wanting to talk
8. being polite
9. doing your share
10. being involved with a team
11. working with people you don't know

Worksheet #18: Handling Competition

Answer Key:

1. working cooperatively
2. sharing a project

3. standing up for beliefs

4. picking an alternative activity

5. using common sense

Worksheet #19: Managing a Social Life

Answer Key:

Monday: skip the movie, it's a school night

Tuesday: busy day, but no time set aside for studying

Wednesday: another late night

Thursday: skipping school?

Friday: busy day, but seems manageable

Saturday: a fun day

Sunday: hope he can catch up on everything

Worksheet #20: Asking for Help

Answer Key:

1. C; 2. A; 3. B; 4. B

Name_____   Date _____

Getting Along with Teachers
or Authority Figures

Which social skills would be important in the following situations involving teachers, principals, and other authority figures that would be encountered at school?

1. Planning your course schedule for next year _____

   _____

2. Eating lunch in the cafeteria _____

   _____

3. Not understanding a teacher's assignment _____

   _____

4. Being in a class and listening to a "boring" lecture _____

   _____

5. Dealing with a teacher who seems to always be in a bad mood _____

   _____

6. Being told to quiet down in the auditorium _____

   _____

7. Being told to quiet down on the bus on your way to school _____

   _____

8. Passing a teacher in the hallway _____

   _____

9. Responding to invitations to work on a committee for your class _____

   _____

10. Being called into the office to report on
    what you saw concerning vandalism
    in the school

    _____

    _____

    _____

    _____

    _____

Getting Along with Peers

What are some typical situations that would involve students and their peers? Use these settings to get you started. Then think about what social skills might be important to have in each.

I'll trade you two bananas for a piece of cake.

Throw in your pudding and it's a deal!

Eating in the cafeteria _____

_____

_____

_____

_____

In P.E. class in the gymnasium _____

_____

At a game _____

_____

In the hallway _____

_____

Riding the bus_____

_____

Sitting in the front of the room _____

_____

Sitting next to someone you like _____

_____

Sitting next to someone you don't like _____

_____

Working on a small group project _____

_____

Participating in after-school sports _____

_____

Doing volunteer projects for a class _____

_____

Name_____ Date _____

Handling Competition

How are these students handling competition by using good social skills?

1. "Let's help each other practice. I'll time you while you run the mile, then you time me. We'll both improve—hopefully!"

_____
_____
_____
_____

2. "It doesn't make sense for both of us to do the biography report on the same person. Why don't you take the early years of her life and I'll take the later years? Then we'll be judged on different aspects."

_____
_____
_____
_____

3. "I'm sorry, but I'm not going to cheat on the Math Competition to have my team win. We'll win anyway, because we're better!!!"

_____
_____
_____
_____

4. "It doesn't seem likely that I would make cheerleading—I know I'm not very coordinated. I'll never beat out all those other girls. So maybe I should sign up for the Pep Club. That would still be fun and I am better at screaming than doing handsprings!"

_____
_____
_____
_____
_____

5. "The teacher is grading this test "on the curve," so only a few people will get A's. I think I better put in some extra hours studying!"

_____
_____
_____
_____

Name_____ Date _____

Managing a Social Life

What do you think of Jerry's social calendar for this week? Does he need to make any changes? What would you suggest?

Monday

7:30 class committee meets to work on Spring Dance idea
noon eat with Debbie in cafeteria
3:00 meet with counselor to plan bulletin board for hallway
4:00 baseball practice
6:00 to the movies with Norm, Joey, and Tom
9:00 study with Arnie
Suggestion: _____

Tuesday

6:00 jogging with Bob
7:30 class committee meets for breakfast
noon eat with Sandy in cafeteria
3:30 work out at the YMCA with the guys
5:00 stop by nursing home to see grandma
6:00 dinner with family
7:30 return phone calls to friends
9:00 watch TV movie with Steve
Suggestion: _____

Wednesday

6:00 jogging with Bob
7:30 class committee meets to work on Spring Dance decorations
noon eat with Alicia in cafeteria
3:00 Math Whiz Club meets
4:00 baseball practice
6:30 volunteer at Animal Shelter
8:00 dinner with new girl in class

Thursday

6:00 leave for amusement park with the guys
9:00 collapse!
Suggestion: _____

Friday

6:00 jogging with Bob
7:30 meet with class committee to work on decorations
noon eat with Yolanda in cafeteria
4:00 baseball game
7:30 dinner with the team
Suggestion: _____

Saturday

6:00 A.M.-10:00 P.M. all-day field trip with baseball team to major league baseball game
Suggestion: _____

Sunday

sleep in, do homework, do laundry
Suggestion: _____

© 1998 by John Wiley & Sons, Inc.

Name_____ Date _____

Asking for Help

What social skill does each student below need to work on in order to effectively ask for help?

    A. Being a Good Listener

    B. Being Able to Communicate

    C. Being Able to Assess a Situation

    D. Using Common Sense

Social Skills Applied at School
Problems or Unusual Situations

INSTRUCTOR PAGE

Introduction: School can be a place where social survival is often an ongoing battle. Peer pressure, pressure from teachers, and "fitting in" are important issues that confront students daily. These worksheets involve considering situations that are difficult or problematic at school.

WORKSHEETS

Note: Answers to the worksheets will vary according to the ages and developmental stages of your students. The answers provided in the Answer Keys are models for typical responses you should expect from your students. As with any other activity, accept answers that can be logically supported by facts.

Worksheet #21: Failing Classes

Answer Key:

1. listen more carefully, take notes

2. share the load

3. stay home and get your work done first

4. realize that you may not do well on that one test; realize that each grade is important

Worksheet #22: Discipline Problems

Answer Key:

1. C; 2. D; 3. A; 4. B

Worksheet #23: Intimidation from Other Students

Answer Key:

The student first tried to defend herself, but—realizing she was getting nowhere—she decided to leave. This is a healthy decision in this social situation!

Worksheet #24: Feeling Like a Misfit

Answer Key:

The first student revealed that he probably wouldn't do well, but was interested in trying anyway. The friend was supportive and encouraging. Without the knowledge, the second person may not have gotten to know the first person.

Worksheet #25: Asking for Help

Answer Key:

1. "A good education will help you get a job."

2. "Are you asking questions if you don't understand?"

3. "Don't let others ruin your opportunity—or be an excuse!"

4. "Ask for extra credit, do independent projects."

5 "Plan to be awake when the instruction is available."

6. "Is that your life goal?"

7. "What if you start missing more than you can handle?"

8. "That shows lack of effort; what does that say about you as a worker?"

Name_____ Date _____

Failing Classes

These students are having difficulty in their classes at school. How could these social skills help them do better?

1. Being a Good Listener

I never seem to know what my assignments are or when they are due.

_____

_____

_____

_____

2. Working with Others

I know we were supposed to work on the project as a group, but I was too busy, so I guess I didn't turn in my share.

_____

_____

_____

_____

3. Reacting Appropriately to Peer Pressure

I would much rather go out with my friends than stay home on a weekend and study! Come on!

_____

_____

_____

_____

4. Being Able to Assess a Situation

I don't care if I get an F on a quiz. All I have to do is get a high enough grade on the final to pass.

_____

_____

_____

_____

Name_____ Date _____

Worksheet #22

Discipline Problems

What skill(s) might help the following students get along in matters of discipline at school?

A. Reacting Properly to Peer Pressure   B. Developing a Good Reputation

C. Controlling Emotions   D. Using Common Sense

1.

Well, I have another detention after school for talking back to the teacher, but I don't care. I told him off!!!

2.

Another write-up for not having my assignment done? Again! I'm just going to tear it up. I'm not going to do it. I don't care if I get in trouble.

3.

Johnny and I are planning to fight those creeps after school. We just have to stay off of school property and we'll be okay.

4.

I can't believe I got in trouble for using swear words. Everybody swears around here. Why should I get in trouble for that?

© 1998 by John Wiley & Sons, Inc.

Worksheet #23 **Intimidation from Other Students**

How did this student handle this situation in which another student tried to intimidate her? What skills did she use?

Answer:

_____

_____

_____

_____

_____

_____

_____

_____

_____

Worksheet #24

Feeling Like a Misfit

How did this student use the social skill *Revealing Yourself to Others* to help himself fit in?

Answer:

_____

_____

_____

_____

_____

_____

_____

_____

Name_____ Date _____

Developing a Bad Attitude
Toward School

Read these comments that reflect a bad attitude toward
school. What advice might you give to each person?

ZZZZZZ

1. School is stupid. What does it do for anyone anyhow?

   _____

   _____

2. These teachers are so dumb—they don't care if we do
   well or not. No one tries to explain anything so you
   understand it.

   _____

   _____

3. How can you learn anything when there are gangs and drugs and kids who don't know how to
   behave in your classes? It makes me want to quit.

   _____

   _____

4. I'm really smart, and I resent it when the stupid kids in the class slow us down.

   _____

   _____

5. I don't really wake up until after lunch, so whatever happens in my morning classes is wasted
   on me!

   _____

   _____

6. I can't wait to quit school. I'm going to work at a gas station and make some real money pumping
   gas!

   _____

   _____

7. It doesn't matter if I miss a day or two each week. I can get the assignments and make them up.

   _____

   _____

8. All I have to do is pass my classes. I don't care if I get A's—I just can't get any F's. I'll do the
   minimum amount of work I have to do to get by!!

   _____

   _____

Social Skills Applied at School
Enhancing the School Situation

INSTRUCTOR PAGE

Introduction: Not everyone is an excellent student, but anyone can make the effort to be outstanding in some way. These worksheets involve having students consider how they can be a part of making the school experience a positive one.

WORKSHEETS

Note: Answers to the worksheets will vary according to the ages and developmental stages of your students. The answers provided in the Answer Keys are models for typical responses you should expect from your students. As with any other activity, accept answers that can be logically supported by facts.

Worksheet #26: Getting Involved in Extracurricular Activities

Answer Key:

grandparent's day; tour guide for new students; organize banquet for school volunteers

Worksheet #27: Being Part of a Team

Answer Key:

being a good listener, understanding another's point of view, being able to communicate, having a sense of humor, using common sense, etc.

Worksheet #28: Putting Forth Extra Effort Towards Excellence

Answer Key:

1. add length, references, visual aids
2. make a poster
3. have an interesting cover that will catch the reader's attention
4. take candid photographs of students at school, have framed, make a poster, etc.
5. slow down, be extra careful
6. do the best job at being a manager, cheer for the team, no complaining
7. use bright colors, do a rough draft first, be neat, label the states accurately and clearly
8. have placemats and napkins, flowers on the tables, etc.

Worksheet #29: Helping Others at School

Answer Key:

1. go with George to talk to the teacher; understanding another's point of view
2. help her get organized; working with others
3. try out with her; maintaining friendships
4. choose Alberto; initiating positive contacts
5. try to talk the girls out of it; reacting to peer pressure
6. tutor Rick; reading other's moods
7. initiate a friendship with Megan; initiating positive contacts
8. use humor to help them pay attention; using humor appropriately

Worksheet #30: Demonstrating School Spirit

Answer Key:

1. be a good sport
2. dance with lots of people
3. don't litter
4. clean up the hallways
5. wear school colors on game days
6. make a bulletin board for your club or group
7. announce upcoming events
8. join in community projects
9. let the community know what is going on
10. raise money for club or project
11. invite other students over to see your school
12. participate—be a good example
13. attend and find out what's been happening
14. collect autographs, write interesting comments in others' books

Name_____ Date _____

Getting Involved in
Extracurricular Activities

What extracurricular activities are available at your school? What are some activities that you would like to see added? How do these activities make school a more pleasant social place for students?

- sports

- art club

- drama club

- school play

- foreign language club

- working on the yearbook

- volunteering at the hospital

- volunteering at a nursing home

- pep club

- manager of a sports team

- chess club

- painting murals on the wall

- peer tutoring

- tutoring younger children

Can you name any other activities?

_____

_____

_____

_____

_____

Being Part of a Team

How can being part of an organized team help develop social skills?

Answer:

_____

_____

_____

Putting Forth Extra Effort
Towards Excellence

How could these students strive toward excellence—going beyond what is expected—in these situations?

My masterpiece!

1. Tonya got a C+ on her research report. It is five pages long and she only used one reference. There are no pictures.

   _____

   _____

2. Ming is giving an oral report on an inventor. He is supposed to give a 3- to 5-minute report with at least one visual aid.

   _____

3. Arthur has written a creative story. He plans to have his sister type it up so it will be easy to read.

   _____

4. Colleen is taking a photography class. She is supposed to turn in 12 photos in some sort of display.

   _____

5. Marcos helps the school janitor clean up the cafeteria after meals. He usually hurries through his job.

   _____

6. Kara is one of the managers for the girls' basketball team. She is responsible for scorekeeping, getting water for the players, and running errands. She wishes she had made the team, since several of her friends did.

   _____

7. Will's social studies teacher asked him to design and paint a map of the United States on the wall.

   _____

8. Amy's home economics group is preparing a tea for the teachers during Appreciation Week. She is supposed to plan activities for this event.

   _____

Name_____ Date _____

Helping Others at School

How could you be helpful to others in the following situations? What social skills might be used?

1. George is having a personality conflict with the science teacher. He is afraid he will get an unfair grade.

   _____

2. Sandy is so disorganized that she loses her assignments almost immediately after finishing them and then has to re-do them to get credit. You, on the other hand, are always well-organized!

   _____

3. Toni really would like to try out for the volleyball team, but she isn't sure she is good enough and doesn't want to make a fool of herself.

   _____

4. No one has chosen Alberto to be part of a cooperative group in health class. He's new to the town and doesn't really know anyone yet.

   _____

5. Kim is always bragging about how good she is at everything—whether she is or not! You find out about some girls planning to make sure she gets in trouble in P.E. class.

   _____

6. Rick has the hardest time catching on to fractions in math class. He seems so slow! You know he is getting discouraged.

   _____

7. Megan has a physical disability and is in a wheelchair. Although she doesn't feel sorry for herself, a lot of other people don't know how to act around her so they leave her alone.

   _____

8. Mrs. Tune, the choir teacher, wants to try putting on a play with the class, but a lot of the students are rowdy and not listening to her directions.

   _____

   _____

Demonstrating School Spirit

What are some ways you could show support or loyalty for your school in the following situations?

- sports events _____

    _____

- school dances_____

    _____

- outside appearance of the school _____

    _____

- inside appearance of the school _____

    _____

- clothing that you wear _____

    _____

- bulletin boards _____

    _____

- ads in the newspaper _____

    _____

- community projects _____

    _____

- local TV or radio announcements_____

    _____

- bake sale/car wash projects _____

    _____

- "sister" schools in other states or countries _____

    _____

- school theater or choir performances _____

    _____

- reunions _____

    _____

    _____

- class yearbooks _____

    _____

    _____

Social Skills Applied at Work
Routine Situations

INSTRUCTOR PAGE

Introduction: Work is a part of life. In this section, students are given routine situations to think through, situations they might encounter in a typical job setting.

WORKSHEETS

Note: Answers to the worksheets will vary according to the ages and developmental stages of your students. The answers provided in the Answer Keys are models for typical responses you should expect from your students. As with any other activity, accept answers that can be logically supported by facts.

Worksheet #31: Getting Along With Your Supervisor

Answer Key:

1. being able to communicate
2. understanding another's point of view
3. being a good listener
4. reading other's moods
5. making a good impression
6. reacting appropriately to peer pressure

Worksheet #32: Getting Along With Co-workers

Answer Key:

1. negotiating or compromising
2. being able to assess a situation
3. working with others
4. making healthy decisions in social situations
5. being flexible
6. working with others

Worksheet #33: Understanding the Skills Required for the Job

Answer Key:

1. being responsible, liking kids
2. showing up on time, having equipment
3. knowing how to operate the machine
4. following directions
5. knowledge of bike parts, careful attention to detail
6. listening to instructions, showing up on time
7. typing accurately
8. knowing locations of houses or knowing how to read a map
9. having equipment, knowing a weed from a flower
10. being polite, listening to orders, making suggestions
11. following instructions, attention to safety rules for frying
12. knowing the alphabet, filing carefully

Worksheet #34: Developing Good Work Habits

Answer Key:

1. yes; making good impression
2. no; needs to be more organized
3. no; needs to react appropriately to peer pressure
4. yes; working with others
5. no; impolite
6. no; needs to make good impression
7. yes; being flexible
8. yes; compromising

Worksheet #35: Following Instructions

Answer Key:

1. hard to make change, unsafe to take large bills
2. someone might steal
3. the boss won't consider an incomplete application
4. you might pass on germs
5. a child could get hit by a car
6. you could get behind in your work
7. your car might get towed
8. customers will appreciate the sale, especially if you call attention to sale items
9. you will know what problems the customers are having
10. the manager or accountant needs to balance the day's transactions

Name_____   Date _____

Worksheet #31 **Getting Along with Your Supervisor**

What social skills might be helpful in dealing with the following situations at work?

1. Your supervisor just made out the work schedule for the week and got your hours all mixed up. You thought you had told him when you were available, but apparently he didn't hear or understand you. The whole schedule will have to be redone.

_____

_____

2. You have a new supervisor on your job. He doesn't really know what everyone is supposed to be doing yet, and you realize that he is making some mistakes on orders.

_____

_____

3. Your supervisor wants you to learn how to do a new job on the computer. She isn't explaining things very well, and you aren't sure that you are interested in learning this anyway—but you want to keep your job!

_____

_____

4. Mornings seem to be a bad time for everyone at your workplace, but especially your boss. She arrives in a very bad mood every morning which makes everyone else fearful and unsure.

_____

_____

5. There is going to be an inspection at your workplace tomorrow, so your supervisor wants everything to be in really good shape. She asks you to stay late to help her get things ready, although you had other plans.

_____

_____

6. No one seems to like the supervisor. In fact, some of the employees are planning to call in sick on the same day so he will have a really hard time getting through the day. You know about it, but aren't sure if you want to be a part of it.

_____

_____

Worksheet #32   # Getting Along with Co-workers

What social skills might help each person below get along with the people he or she has to work with?

1. *Can someone change shifts with me? I've got a huge term paper due next week and could really use the extra time to study!*

_____
_____

2. *I think Gina is picking up your tips from the tables you're waiting on.*

_____
_____
_____

3. *Someone should talk to Theo about getting to work on time. He's late every morning and we have to get the breakfast orders out!*

_____
_____
_____

4. *Amy is really nice to work with, but she doesn't do a very good job. I have to go over everything she does and re-do it.*

_____
_____
_____

5. *Everyone has to do their share and then some, because it's going to be a busy party tonight. Don't wait to be told what to do—if you see something that needs to be done, do it!*

_____
_____
_____

6. *We can get a raise after six months if we are doing a good job. We can help each other look good!*

_____
_____
_____

Name_____ Date _____

Understanding the Skills
Required for the Job

What skills might be required in order to perform the following jobs well?

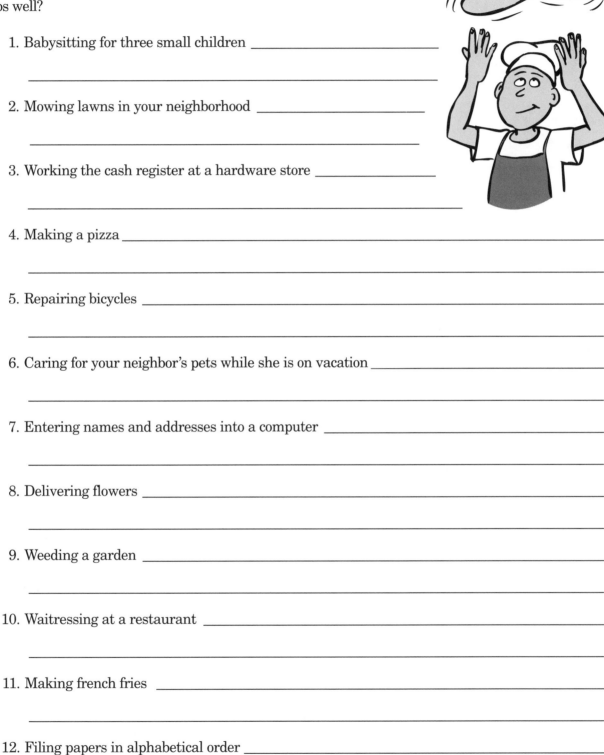

1. Babysitting for three small children _____

_____

2. Mowing lawns in your neighborhood _____

_____

3. Working the cash register at a hardware store _____

_____

4. Making a pizza _____

_____

5. Repairing bicycles _____

_____

6. Caring for your neighbor's pets while she is on vacation _____

_____

7. Entering names and addresses into a computer _____

_____

8. Delivering flowers _____

_____

9. Weeding a garden _____

_____

10. Waitressing at a restaurant _____

_____

11. Making french fries _____

_____

12. Filing papers in alphabetical order _____

_____

Name_____ Date _____

Developing Good Work Habits

Which of these characters are demonstrating good work habits? What social skills have they developed?

1.  Good morning, welcome to Frank's Restaurant. May I help you find a place to sit? Would you like to be by a window?

_____

2.  Sorry I'm late. My car was out of gas again.

_____

3. Come on—leave work early and go out with us! Okay, I'll tell the boss I'm feeling sick. Count me in!

_____

4.  Well, my work station is all clean and organized now. The next person shouldn't have any trouble finding anything.

_____

5. What do you mean, you ordered LARGE fries? You did not. Take these.

_____

6. I wore this shirt yesterday, but I think it's still okay to wear to work today.

_____

7. Ooh—this window is filthy! I'll get some rags and take care of it.

_____

8. I'm sorry, Mr. Jones, but I have another orthodontist appointment on Friday so I'll have to leave early. However, I'll be more than happy to work this weekend or put in extra hours when you need somebody on another day. . .

_____
_____

Name_____ Date _____

Following Instructions

Read the following instructions that might be given while on the job. What problems might occur if they were not followed?

Yeah? And then what did she say? Well, you know what I think!? Blah. . . blah. . . blah. . .

Instructions:

1. Don't take any bills over $20. _____

_____

_____

_____

2. Lock the safe at 11 P.M. _____

_____

3. Fill out names and addresses completely for people who you are using as references on your job application.

_____

_____

4. Wash your hands before handling food. _____

_____

5. Don't let children cross the street except at the light._____

_____

6. No personal phone calls are allowed while working._____

_____

7. Employees should park only in special parking areas._____

_____

8. All merchandise with a red tag on it is 50% off today. _____

_____

9. Ask all customers to fill out comment cards._____

_____

10. Turn in all of your receipts each evening before you leave. _____

_____

Social Skills Applied at Work

Problems or Unusual Situations

INSTRUCTOR PAGE

Introduction: Every work situation has its own set of problems that must be addressed. Possessing good social skills can allow a worker to work through these situations.

WORKSHEETS

Note: Answers to the worksheets will vary according to the ages and developmental stages of your students. The answers provided in the Answer Keys are models for typical responses you should expect from your students. As with any other activity, accept answers that can be logically supported by facts.

Worksheet #36: Dealing With an Unfair Boss

Answer Key:

1. ask for more notice; negotiating or compromising
2. mention that you've done it for three days; being able to communicate
3. don't argue; being able to assess a situation
4. ask for more specific expectations; being a good listener
5. tell him you can't do it; standing up for your beliefs
6. tell how you feel; revealing yourself to others

Worksheet #37: Working With Annoying Co-workers

Answer Key:

1. talk to co-worker about problem; understanding another's point of view
2. ask why she doesn't move on; controlling emotions
3. not doing her job; standing up for your beliefs
4. ask him to tone down his language; standing up for your beliefs
5. comment that you're not as intelligent; having a sense of humor
6. tell him to listen better; being able to communicate

Worksheet #38: Dealing With Complaining Customers

Answer Key:

1. negotiating or compromising
2. having a good reputation
3. understanding another's point of view
4. reading other's moods
5. controlling emotions
6. understanding another's point of view

Worksheet #39: Lack of Respect from Your Employees

Answer Key:

1. say, "I guess no one wants a bonus this week."
2. it might be time to fire some employees
3. stop lending it out—or ask for a damage deposit

4. compliment the ones who are working well

5. reveal your feelings—enough is enough

6. have them sign in to use one phone for personal calls—if they find they are being monitored, they may cut down

Worksheet #40: Bringing Personal Problems to Work

Answer Key:

1. be friendly and say, "Hi! Well, you can see I've come up in the world!"

2. don't harass her—think before you act

3. think about what you do know, concentrate, clear your head

4. agree to split the project—let Mandy choose first what she wants to do

5. tell Marcos to respect your position at work—and learn from this experience!

Dealing with an Unfair Boss

How could you handle the following situations in which the boss seems to be unfair? What social skills could you use?

1.

"I know I didn't give you any notice, but don't bother coming in next week to work. My cousins are in town and I'm going to keep them busy."

_____
_____
_____

2.

"Jaime and Paul can work the desk today. George, you can clean up the trash around the building. I know you did it for the last three days, but you're doing a good job of it."

_____
_____
_____
_____

3.
"I know I told you that you were supposed to clock in before you start work. I don't know why you're saying I didn't tell you. Of course I must have told you."

_____
_____
_____

4.
"This counter isn't clean! Clean it again!! It's pitiful!"

_____
_____
_____

5.
"We need extra help around here on Sunday. I put you down for a 12-hour shift. You can study for your exams in between customers, I guess."

SUNDAY

_____
_____
_____

6.
"You were late to work again today, so I'm docking your pay for an hour. I know you had to park three blocks away, but you should have thought of that and left for work earlier."

_____
_____

Name_____ Date _____

Working with Annoying Co-workers

How are these co-workers annoying? What could you do to resolve the situations? What social skills might help you?

1.

Sorry I'm late again! Don't tell the boss, okay?

_____
_____
_____

2.

I hate this job. I'm just here for the money. This job really stinks. What a bore. I'm so much better than this.

_____
_____
_____

3.

I have to use the phone again, so would you take care of that customer for me? I'll just be a second.

_____
_____
_____

4.

Pass me the *&(#*& pen, would you? I have to fill out the)(*&(*&(report. It just takes so *&(*&(long to do all this paperwork!

_____
_____
_____

5.

Well, I never have any trouble working with that machine. It never gives ME any problems. You must just not know how to use it.

_____
_____
_____

6.

What did the boss tell us to do? When is this supposed to be done? Did you catch what he said about what clothes to wear? Huh?

_____
_____
_____

Name_____ Date _____

Dealing with Complaining Customers

What social skill(s) did the following characters use to handle customers with complaints?

1.   *This food is cold! Take it back!*      *How about if I make sure you get a free dessert to make up for this?*

_____

_____

2.   *This model is missing some parts.*      *That's really unusual! Our company stands behind its products and sales. We'll make it right, don't worry.*

_____

_____

3.   *I don't like the color of this watch band. It's really awful.*       *You know, red is not my favorite color either. I can understand why you don't like it.*

_____

_____

4.   *You were late to my house to take the dogs out.*   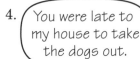   *Well, you told me 8 a.m. and that's what time I got there. Perhaps I should come at 7:30 tomorrow instead. . . ?*

_____

_____

5.   *I have been waiting in line for 15 minutes! Everyone is moving too slowly!*      *(I want to slug her!!!) Well, I am sorry about your wait. There are a lot of people here. I'll work as quickly as I can!*

_____

_____

6.   *This soda doesn't have any fizz in it! Your machines must be defective. Don't you ever check them?*       *It's really hot out today, and I'm sure you must be really thirsty. I'll make sure you get something nice and cold. Hang on!*

_____

_____

Name_____ Date _____

Lack of Respect from Your Employees

How could you handle the following situations if YOU were the boss and your employees were giving you a hard time?

1. You have asked your employees to clean up the restaurant before the breakfast customers begin to come in. After you leave to answer the phone, you find that they are all sitting in the booths, talking, laughing, and playing cards!

   _____

   _____

2. You are in charge of scheduling help in the clothing store for the weekend. After taking into consideration everyone's other plans for the weekend, you came up with a schedule that seems to be fair for everyone. When Friday night comes, however, people begin calling in that they can't come in to work that weekend.

   _____

   _____

3. You have been renting out your lawn mower to your friends who are trying to get some extra money during the summer doing yardwork. Although you have asked them to keep the lawn mower clean and let you know if anything isn't working right, they keep returning it to you and it doesn't work properly.

   _____

   _____

4. You are responsible for supervising a group of older kids who are reading to younger kids. As long as you watch them, they do well—but when you're not right there, the older kids are goofing around.

   _____

   _____

5. You are a senior counselor at Camp Lotza Funn. The junior counselors keep playing tricks on you, such as messing up your room, putting signs on your back, and putting pepper in your food. It was funny at first, but after your underwear was run up the flagpole, you quickly became tired of all this.

   _____

   _____

6. The rules about using the phone at work are clear and posted, but when you are the one in charge of the office, the employees rush for the phone to make all kinds of personal phone calls. You get the feeling that if you tell on them to YOUR supervisor, things will be even more difficult for you, yet you are responsible for keeping things going when you're in charge.

   _____

   _____

Name_____ Date _____

Bringing Personal Problems to Work

How might using these social skills help you resolve situations in which you bring personal problems to work?

1. Using Humor Appropriately

Oh no—there's my old boyfriend! I'm too embarrassed to wait on him! What'll I do?

_____
_____
_____
_____

2. Controlling Emotions

I'm so upset about my best friend using drugs. I just want to scream! It really bothers me!

_____
_____
_____
_____

3. Being Able to Assess a Situation

I should have studied last night for that test. I'm going to flunk it, I just know it!

_____
_____
_____
_____

4. Being Flexible

I hate working with Mandy! She never does her share and she's so nasty and snotty to me! I don't think I can work with her!!

_____
_____
_____
_____

5. Developing a Good Reputation

I'm afraid Marcos is going to come by and tell everybody how drunk I was last night at the party. I don't want my boss to find out. . .

_____
_____
_____

Social Skills Applied at Work
Enhancing the Work Situation

INSTRUCTOR PAGE

Introduction: An exceptionally good worker not only makes the workplace more efficient and pleasant, but he or she also demonstrates qualities that can lead to advancement. These worksheets focus on ways in which a worker can be outstanding—not just adequate.

WORKSHEETS

Note: Answers to the worksheets will vary according to the ages and developmental stages of your students. The answers provided in the Answer Keys are models for typical responses you should expect from your students. As with any other activity, accept answers that can be logically supported by facts.

Worksheet #41: Developing an Excellent Performance Record

Answer Key:

1. good attendance reflects interest and commitment to job

2. shows that he is prepared, ready to work

3. conscientious

4. well organized, takes job seriously

5. shows initiative

6. smart; knows how to get a good evaluation that may lead to promotions

Worksheet #42: Demonstrating a Good Attitude

Answer Key:

1. pleasant; making a good impression

2. leadership; being flexible

3. willing to learn; being a good listener

4. not afraid of hard work; being able to assess a situation

5. ability to prioritize; being able to assess a situation

6. thankful; being able to communicate

Worksheet #43: Being Resourceful in Taking Over Other Jobs

Answer Key:

1. prioritizes

2. organized

3. takes initiative

4. ability to assess difficulty of tasks

5. effort was noticed by the boss

Worksheet #44: Making the Boss or Business Look Good

Answer Key:

1. making a good impression

2. making a good impression

3. good reputation; working with others

4. compromising; being flexible

5. negotiating; good reputation

6. good impression; initiating positive contacts

Worksheet #45: Taking Initiative for Promotion

Answer Key:

Answers will vary; the following are examples of typical student responses—

keep up a résumé of your skills and jobs

check the classifieds in your paper

be available for overtime, extra projects

be pleasant—have a good attitude

make sure people know your name

Developing an Excellent Performance Record

How have these characters gone beyond what was probably expected of them to demonstrate an excellent work record?

AWARD TO:

1. **Melanie** for perfect attendance at work two years in a row

   _____

   _____

2. **Jamal** arrives at work 10 to 15 minutes EARLY each day

   _____

   _____

3. **Kim** is the last one to leave, makes SURE everything is done before she goes

   _____

   _____

4. **Darnell** is prepared for all inspections well ahead of time

   _____

   _____

5. **Sandra** asks questions when she doesn't understand how to do something and then finds out how to do it BETTER

   _____

   _____

6. **Elston** knows exactly what he will be evaluated on and has no problem with any aspect of it!

   _____

   _____

Name_____   Date _____

Demonstrating a Good Attitude

How are these workers demonstrating a good attitude on the job? What social skills are they using?

1.

Good morning, everybody! Have a good weekend?

_____

_____

_____

2.

I know we're late on a lot of projects. I'm willing to put in some overtime to get it done.

_____

_____

_____

3.

I can see now that I made some mistakes on this. I'll make sure that I don't do it again and find out exactly what I did wrong.

_____

_____

_____

4.

Some parts of this job are hard, but I'll just look at it as a challenge. I can do it.

_____

_____

_____

5.

What?! The inspection is in 10 minutes? Well, okay. I'll put everything else aside and concentrate on that.

_____

_____

_____

6.

Thank you for letting me know that I'm doing a good job. It's important to me to know that people think highly of me.

_____

_____

_____

Name_____ Date _____

Worksheet #43

Being Resourceful in Taking Over Other Jobs

Suzanna found out that her work partner called in sick and she suddenly had to do other jobs. How does Suzanna demonstrate her resourcefulness?

1. **8:30 A.M.** She is pulled off her regular job and has to fill in for someone else.

_____
_____
_____

I'll put everything on my desk aside that isn't urgent and I'll get to it when I can.

2. **9:00 A.M.** A customer calls in with a complaint that she knows nothing about.

_____
_____
_____

I'm really sorry about this—it seems to be a big mix-up. I'll take all of the information and make sure I get it to a supervisor. I'll do the best I can to try to get this straightened out.

3. **11:30 A.M.** She has to go late to lunch due to her helping to clean up another area of the work station.

_____
_____
_____

Yuck! This hasn't been dusted in weeks! What a mess! Oh well, I'll try to figure out what goes where. . .

4. **1:00 P.M.** After returning from lunch, Suzanna finds out there are lots more problems to solve!

_____
_____
_____

This is the pile of things that will have to go to a supervisor; this is the pile of things I think I can handle; and this is the pile of things I think should be thrown out but I'm not the one to do it!

5. **5:00 P.M.** Suzanna gets ready to leave.

_____
_____
_____

Will Amy be back tomorrow? Please say YES!

Actually, the boss noticed how well you handled everything today and wants to keep you in his department!

Name_____ Date _____

Worksheet #44

Making the Boss or Business Look Good

In what ways are these employees helping the boss or the company look good to others? How are they using the following social skills?

Negotiating or Compromising   Initiating Positive Contacts

Making a Good Impression   Developing a Good Reputation

Working with Others   Being Flexible

1.

This is a really good product. I use it myself at home all the time. It really makes my job easier to know that I believe in what we're making and selling!

2.

Everything is so clean here! Everyone is so friendly! What a nice place to work.

Yes, it is. Thank you.

3.

No one takes individual credit for this—it is a team project. We all contribute our ideas and we all listen to each other's suggestions. We work together.

4.

Well, I just found out that I have to come in on Saturday to work. I had plans, but I know that it's only fair. Someone else had to work last weekend in my place. The job has to get done. I can work it out.

5.

I'm sorry you weren't happy with our product. Would you like us to replace it with something else? Or would you prefer a refund? We'll be glad to do what it takes to make you a satisfied customer. We'll work with you.

6.

Hello and welcome to our restaurant. It's a beautiful day, isn't it? Would you like some coffee while you're looking over the menu? We have some great specials today!

Taking Initiative for Promotion

Here are some ways an employee can try to get a promotion or a better job.

- Find out what other jobs are available.

- Find out what the qualifications are for other jobs.

- Talk to people in the business who would know about other jobs.

- Be sure to get the best personal evaluation for the present job.

- Let your boss know you are interested in taking on new responsibilities.

- Let your boss know you would like to apply for a different job.

- Have good reasons for why you should be considered for a promotion.

- Maintain a good work record at your present job.

- Look for opportunities to learn new skills and get more training.

- Work on having very good social skills!

Can you list some other ways to take initiative for promotion?

1. _____

_____

2. _____

_____

3. _____

_____

4. _____

_____

5. _____

_____

Social Skills Applied with Peers
Routine Situations

INSTRUCTOR PAGE

Introduction: Peers have a powerful impact on what we think, do, and how we feel about things. It is important to feel secure in ourselves as individuals, yet able to relate well to others. These worksheets examine ordinary interactions with others.

WORKSHEETS

Note: Answers to the worksheets will vary according to the ages and developmental stages of your students. The answers provided in the Answer Keys are models for typical responses you should expect from your students. As with any other activity, accept answers that can be logically supported by facts.

Worksheet #46: Respecting Others as Individuals

Answer Key:

1. ask questions about their ethnic background
2. attend a service (wedding, church meeting, etc.)
3. learn some sign language
4. make an effort to be patient
5. don't be critical—find out what he or she is good at
6. treat him or her as any other friend
7. don't call attention to the problem
8. don't act unnatural—be yourself
9. ask questions about what it was like
10. congratulate him or her

Worksheet #47: Recognizing the Value of Friendship

Answer Key:

1. made time for him; listened to him
2. took care of the dog even though it was difficult for her
3. traded favors
4. took responsibility off of friend
5. made sure her friend was okay
6. cheered for friend, helped him train

Worksheet #48: Developing Healthy Relationships With the Opposite Sex

Answer Key:

1. yes—making healthy decisions
2. no
3. no
4. yes—good listener, able to communicate
5. yes—maintaining friendships
6. yes—initiating positive contacts
7. no

8. no

9. yes—initiating positive contacts, making a good impression

10. no

11. yes—reading other's moods

12. yes—healthy decisions in social situations

Worksheet #49: Taking Advantage of Social Opportunities

Answer Key:

1. responding to invitation

2. helping make phone calls

3. meeting someone in the store

4. discussing the dog

5. joining a class

6. having a mutual interest in music

7. sharing a common interest in a TV show

8. taking advantage of opportunity to participate

Worksheet #50: Deciding How Much Influence Others Will Have Over You

Answer Key:

1. responding to peer pressure; standing up for what's more important

2. giving in a little; standing up for beliefs

3. impulsive; more practical—assessing situation

4. ready to form opinion based on another's opinion; making own judgment

5. adhering to goal; ready to change plans

Worksheet #46   # Respecting Others as Individuals

How could you show respect for others in these situations? In what ways could you get to know or understand this person, especially if he or she is very different from you?

1. Someone whose race is different from yours

_____

_____

2. Someone who has different religious beliefs from you

_____

_____

3. Someone who has a hearing impairment

_____

4. Someone who does not speak your language very well

_____

5. Someone who is not a good athlete

_____

6. Someone who is very rich

_____

7. Someone who stutters

_____

8. Someone who is very popular

_____

9. Someone who has appeared on television as a model

_____

10. Someone who wins awards for academic contests

_____

Worksheet #47 **Recognizing the Value of Friendship**

How does each person in the stories below show friendship towards another person? Why would the other person value that friendship?

1. Carlos was very depressed after his father died. It seemed as though he didn't want to go to school or work or do anything that he used to do. Ramon made sure that he called Carlos often and included him in activities. He said that if Carlos ever wanted to talk, he would be around for him. In fact, Ramon's father had died when Ramon was a child, so he knew how it felt to lose someone you cared about.

   _____

   _____

2. Debbie needed a place to keep her dog while her family moved to a new house, or she would have to give it to the animal shelter. Alison was allergic to animals, but said that she'd help take care of the dog until Debbie's family moved into the new house.

   _____

   _____

3. Bonita wanted to go to a party one weekend, but didn't want to go alone. Her friend Sharon had made other plans to work on a school project, but agreed to go with Bonita so she wouldn't have to go alone. In return, Bonita agreed to help Sharon with her project the next day.

   _____

   _____

4. David and Ron worked together at a pizza place. One night David was delayed because he had some family problems to take care of. Ron took over at work and made sure that by the time David got there, everything was under control at work.

   _____

   _____

5. Lynda was always thinking that she was too fat. She was constantly taking diet pills, over-exercising, and making herself sick. At first she didn't want to listen to Annette warn her about the dangers of anorexia or bulimia, but Annette was persistent and finally talked Lynda into seeing a doctor.

   _____

   _____

6. Tony was one of the captains on the track team. His friend, Ben, was not a runner, but always helped Tony train by running with him after school and on weekends and timing him on various distances. Sometimes Ben would ride his bike to help keep up Tony's speed. He was constantly working with Tony, and was just as excited for his friend when he made the state finals in the mile.

   _____

   _____

Name_____ Date _____

Worksheet #48 # Developing Healthy Relationships
with the Opposite Sex

Check (✓) which of these situations are examples of healthy relationships with the opposite sex. What social skills are involved in each?

[ ] 1. spending time together going to sports events with other friends

_____

[ ] 2. going to a party together where you think there will be drinking and drugs

_____

[ ] 3. sneaking out at night to meet with someone whom you know your parents wouldn't like

_____

[ ] 4. calling the other person to talk about school or work

_____

[ ] 5. spending time listening to the other person talk about what's important to him or her

_____

[ ] 6. taking a computer class where you might meet someone with similar interests

_____

[ ] 7. giving up all of your plans with your friends at the last minute to meet someone who might or might not show up to meet you

_____

[ ] 8. going out with someone who has a bad reputation because no one else has asked you to go out at all

_____

[ ] 9. inviting some people you don't know very well to your house for a swimming party with some of your friends

_____

[ ] 10. leaving with someone you just met at a party because he or she seems nice

_____

[ ] 11. spending time getting to know someone who seems quiet and doesn't have a lot of other friends

_____

[ ] 12. deciding that you're not going to get too serious with just one person because you'd still like to get to know other people

_____

Name_____ Date _____

Worksheet #49

Taking Advantage of Social Opportunities

How are these individuals taking advantage of social opportunities that have come up?

1. Would you like to go to the game with us on Friday?  Oh, sure! Thanks for asking.

_____
_____

2. Let's plan a party for everyone who helped with the play. Yes! I'll help make phone calls to invite people.

_____
_____

3. Ketchup . . . ketchup . . . Hi! Do you happen to know where the ketchup is?  Well, I sure do. Do you shop here often?

_____
_____

4. What a pretty dog you have. What kind is it? She's a husky mix. Do you like dogs?

_____
_____

5. Here's a sign-up for people to join an exercise class. It looks like fun. Let's do it!

_____
_____

6. I love to listen to music!  Do you want to go to the dance?

_____
_____

7. Oh good! My favorite TV show is coming on.   I like that one, too. Mind if I watch it with you?

_____
_____

8. The hospital is asking for volunteers to help decorate the halls for Christmas. Let's do it! That might be fun!

_____
_____

Name_____ Date _____

Worksheet #50

Deciding How Much Influence
Others Will Have Over You

How are the following characters demonstrating different reactions to the influence that a peer is trying to have over them?

1. Let's cut school today!

Okay. I'm there!

No—I have a big test coming up. Can't make it this time.

_____
_____
_____

2. Oh, come on, everyone is smoking.

Let me think about it.

No way! I'm not even remotely interested.

_____
_____
_____

3. That dress is really cute!

I don't care how much it costs—I'm going to buy it!

I like it, too, but it's very expensive. I'll look for something I can afford.

_____
_____
_____

4. I heard you were friends with Marcia. You know about her wild reputation, don't you?

What do you know about her that I should know?

I'm making my own judgments.

_____
_____
_____

5. Why would you want to take World History in summer school? You should PLAY in the summer!

Well, I need the credits. I'm not going to be playing this summer!

You're right! I'll take it in the fall.

_____
_____
_____

Social Skills Applied with Peers

Problems or Unusual Situations

INSTRUCTOR PAGE

Introduction: Everyone has difficulty with peer relations at times. This series of worksheets provides students with situations in which negative feelings or actions are a part of peer interactions.

WORKSHEETS

Note: Answers to the worksheets will vary according to the ages and developmental stages of your students. The answers provided in the Answer Keys are models for typical responses you should expect from your students. As with any other activity, accept answers that can be logically supported by facts.

Worksheet #51: Getting Involved With People With Problems

Answer Key:

1. try to intervene on his behalf
2. get others in the group to apply pressure
3. talk to the friend
4. encourage her by talking about her good points
5. offer to quiz him on the material
6. ask if he can think of any alternative plans
7. don't judge without evidence
8. offer to go to the counselor with your friend
9. stay out of his way; talk to your parents
10. tell him to lighten up, he's doing fine

Worksheet #52: Feeling Outcast

Answer Key:

1. offers to contribute strengths
2. creative problem solving
3. defends self
4. stands up for friend
5. goes out of her way to befriend someone else

Worksheet #53: Dealing With Hatred, Prejudice, Belittlement

Answer Key:

1. ignore, don't give a reaction that it hurts
2. say you are sorry they feel so prejudiced
3. ask neighbors for help
4. say that you don't find them humorous
5. ask where they buy their clothes—it's too bad they couldn't find something better
6. state you're sorry they can't see beyond your situation
7. do something else that night
8. talk to an adult, police officer, or other authority figure

Worksheet #54: When a Friend Is in Trouble

Answer Key:

1. offer to go to your friend's parents with her
2. talk to him about your concerns
3. encourage your friend to stay home and try to work things out
4. keep trying
5. go with him to talk to the parents
6. talk to your parents about how they made you feel
7. tell your parents that you need their support and understanding

Worksheet #55: Realizing that People and Situations Change

Answer Key:

1. he could get tutoring to try to improve his grades
2. she could work on making new friends
3. he could trade work for lessons
4. she could look for another job
5. he could work after summer school is over
6. she could get a makeover
7. he could have friends over to his house so his aunt and uncle could get to know them
8. she could get extra help from the English teacher to improve her skills

Getting Involved with People with Problems

How could you deal with these individuals who may have problems in their lives?

1. a friend who is having problems getting along with his teachers at school and may be suspended

_____

2. a classmate who doesn't do his share on group projects

_____

_____

_____

_____

3. a good friend who is starting to hang around with gang members

_____

4. your sister who feels as though no one likes her because she's very quiet

_____

5. your partner for science lab who never bothers to read the assignment or seems to understand what to do

_____

6. a friend who is planning to get into a fight with another student because of false rumors that he's spreading around

_____

7. a classmate whom everyone suspects of stealing

_____

8. a friend of yours who is fearfully living with an alcoholic stepfather

_____

9. an older brother who has a very bad temper that seems to be getting worse all the time

_____

10. a friend who gets very upset when he doesn't get an A+ on every assignment

_____

Name_____ Date _____

Feeling Outcast

Sometimes you may feel as though everyone is against you or that you are different or not so good as everyone else. How have these individuals attempted to handle those situations?

1. *Oh, no, are you in our group?*

   Hey, I'm ready to work with you on the project. Maybe I could draw some pictures to go with the presentation.

   _____

   _____

   _____

2. *Everyone choose a partner for basketball.*

   Could we be a group of three?

   _____

   _____

   _____

3. *Look at that hair—when's the last time you touched it? Or do you have lice again?*

   If you don't like the way I look or dress, just look at somebody else. Don't you have anything better to do?

   _____

   _____

   _____

4. *Get the bug spray—Paula was here.*

   I really find it offensive when you are so unkind to people. Words can hurt. Someday you will know how it feels. Good-bye.

   _____

   _____

   _____

5. *I could go through the entire day and not one person would notice me or say a word to me. I'm sure feeling sorry for myself. There's Amy . . . she's all by herself at the lunch table.*

   Hi, Amy. Would you like some company?

   _____

   _____

   _____

Name_____   Date _____

Dealing with Hatred, Prejudice, Belittlement

Unfortunately, some people resort to comments and deeds of hatred and prejudice to express their feelings. If you are a victim of these types of behaviors, what are some possible ways you could react (or act) without retaliating in the same way?

1. making comments about your racial background

   _____

2. using derogatory words about your nationality

   _____

3. putting offensive objects or signs in your yard

   _____

4. telling jokes that make fun of you or your race/sex/nationality

   _____

5. wearing T-shirts with offensive comments on them in front of you

   _____

6. making faces, gestures, or comments directed at you

   _____

7. inviting everyone to a social event except you and your group

   _____

8. making threatening comments or acts towards you and your group

   _____

Name_____ Date _____

When a Friend Is in Trouble

What could you do or say to help a friend if he or she were in serious trouble or experiencing a problem? Consider the following situations.

1. Your friend thinks she is pregnant. The father is someone with a bad reputation who will probably deny the whole thing.

   _____

2. Your friend has started using some recreational drugs. He doesn't seem to care much about school or even work anymore.

   _____

3. Your friend is having a lot of problems at home since his parents' divorce. In fact, he is thinking about running away or possibly moving in with a relative in another state.

   _____

4. Your friend is being given some bad advice from another friend—but when you try to set her straight, your friend won't believe you. You're frustrated that your friend won't listen to you.

   _____

5. Your friend borrowed his parents' car without permission and put a huge dent in the front of it, got a speeding ticket, and is now afraid to go home.

   _____

6. Your friend is a different race than you, and your parents are not willing to accept her as a guest in their house. You are embarrassed and upset by your parents' behavior, but what can you do? Your friend feels hurt and upset.

   _____

7. Your friend lied to her parents about where she was last night—she said she was with YOU. You know that she will get in a lot of trouble if she's caught in a lie. You also know that her parents will be talking to your parents.

   _____

Realizing that People and Situations Change

Time and events can cause many things to change. What are some possible changes that might occur in the following situations?

1. Antonio is afraid he won't get accepted to college because he got a D and a few C's on his latest report card.

   _____

2. Amy is devastated because her best friend since first grade, Delia, is moving to another state.

   _____

3. Carlos has always wanted to learn to play a guitar, but he doesn't have the money for lessons.

   _____

4. Elaine hates her job, cleaning houses after school and on weekends, but she needs the money.

   _____

5. Frank likes helping his uncle build houses in the summer, but it looks as though he'll have to go to summer school instead this year.

   _____

6. Susan feels she isn't very pretty. She doesn't like her glasses, is a little overweight, and cuts her own hair. She wears her older sister's old clothes that don't fit her very well.

   _____

   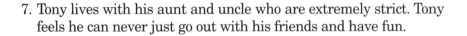

7. Tony lives with his aunt and uncle who are extremely strict. Tony feels he can never just go out with his friends and have fun.

   _____

8. Kara desperately wants to work on the school yearbook, but her English teacher did not recommend her because of her poor writing skills.

   _____

Social Skills Applied with Peers
Enhancing Social Situations with Peers

INSTRUCTOR PAGE

Introduction: Some people are extremely likeable and outgoing—the center of attention and loving every second of it. While most of us may not need or even want so much attention, it is nice to be able to relate well to others by developing some higher level social skills.

WORKSHEETS

Note: Answers to the worksheets will vary according to the ages and developmental stages of your students. The answers provided in the Answer Keys are models for typical responses you should expect from your students. As with any other activity, accept answers that can be logically supported by facts.

Worksheet #56: Choosing to Befriend Someone

Answer Key:

1. giving up time with friends to make a new friend
2. including someone in activities
3. inviting someone to use his skills
4. offering a ride to someone
5. going out of her way to be encouraging

Worksheet #57: Becoming a Good Conversationalist

Answer Key:

1. ask if they have seen the new museum exhibit in town
2. ask if they are going to the game
3. say hello to your neighbors
4. ask if other patients have seen the news that day
5. ask what's the latest style
6. welcome them and ask if they need help finding anything
7. ask if there is anything they need
8. talk about your job skills
9. ask where he moved from
10. talk about the fun activities campers had last year
11. welcome patients
12. ask if it's a special occasion

Worksheet #58: Putting Needs of Others First

Answer Key:

1. letting the person check out first—save her time
2. helping the boy get across
3. offering to help the boy study
4. including Wendy in the party

Worksheet #59: Sticking Up for Those Who Need a Hand

Answer Key:

1. tell them it's none of their business
2. talk to a teacher or counselor to intervene
3. have your dad go to the supervisor to explain the situation
4. tell the other students to grow up
5. warn your sister to be careful not to get hurt
6. encourage your friend to apologize

Worksheet #60: Sharing What Is Important

Answer Key:

1. sharing love of creativity
2. sharing time with kids
3. sharing sports interests/lessons
4. sharing bikes
5. emphasizing likenesses, not differences
6. sharing feelings

Name_____ Date _____

Choosing to Befriend Someone

How are these characters "going the extra mile" to become a friend to someone?

1.

   Jeanne's all by herself again. I'd really like to go out with my friends, but I think Jeanne would appreciate someone spending time with her. I can see my friends later.

   _____
   _____
   _____
   _____

2.

   Hey, would you like to play some football with us in the park after school? It's just for fun.

   _____
   _____
   _____
   _____

3.

   We need an artist to help us with the yearbook cover. Paul, you're really good at drawing. Why don't you come to the meeting tonight?

   _____
   _____
   _____
   _____

4.

   Larry, need a ride? We've got room. Come on.

   _____
   _____
   _____
   _____

5.

   Hi, Mara. I just had a few minutes and thought I'd call to see how that test went that you were worried about.

   _____
   _____
   _____
   _____

Name_____ Date _____

Becoming a Good Conversationalist

What are some ways you can strike up a conversation with someone in these situations?

1. sitting next to someone on a public bus

_____

2. walking along the hall at school with a person you don't know

_____

3. taking your dog for a walk through your
   neighborhood

_____

4. waiting in the dentist's office

_____

5. getting your hair cut at a salon

_____

6. working at the visitor's booth at your church

_____

7. visiting elderly people at a nursing home

_____

8. applying for a job at the local newspaper office

_____

9. making a new student feel welcome

_____

10. answering questions at a summer day camp for children

_____

11. working as a receptionist in a busy doctor's office

_____

12. delivering flowers for a local florist

_____

Name_____ Date _____

Worksheet #58   # Putting Needs of Others First

How are these characters putting the needs of others first?

1.

> What a long line. I'll be here all day. That woman only has two items and seems to be in a hurry.

> Would you like to go ahead of me?

_____
_____
_____
_____

2.

> That little boy can't get across that busy street by himself.

> Here, we're going the same way. Why don't you walk with me?

_____
_____
_____
_____

3.

> I just can't figure this out. I'll just get an F.

> I'm SO busy—I've got my own homework to do.

> Well, I know how to figure that out. I can show you in study hall.

_____
_____
_____
_____

4.

> I love dancing! This party is so much fun! But poor Wendy—nobody is even talking to her.

> Hi, Wendy! Have you tried the new chips yet? Come with me. We must visit the kitchen. Besides, there's someone I want you to meet.

_____
_____
_____
_____

Name_____ Date _____

Sticking Up for Those
Who Need a Hand

It may be hard to stand up for someone else, especially if you might be laughed at or made fun of. How could you stand up for someone who needed help in these situations?

1. Alison is having personal problems at home and is seeing a counselor. Some of her classmates found out and are telling people that she is mentally ill and spreading vicious rumors about her.

_____

2. Lin is from Japan and happens to be an excellent student. Some of the kids are jealous of her and her abilities, so they have started making fun of her nationality.

_____

3. Larry has to work two jobs to help pay for his car and insurance. One weekend he has a conflict in his work schedule and can't make it to both jobs. His boss at one of the jobs will fire him if he doesn't show up. You can't work his job for him, but your father also works at this second job and might have some influence.

_____

4. There are two mentally handicapped students in your P.E. class. Some of the other students make fun of the way they talk and some of the comments they make in class.

_____

5. Your sister's boyfriend wants to break up with her—and everyone seems to know except for your sister, who just bought a prom dress and is expecting to go with him. You have already seen this boy out with other girls. You feel badly for your sister.

_____

6. Your friend made some embarrassing comments about other people at a party when he didn't know he was being videotaped. Now that videotape is being circulated for everyone to look at and laugh at. A lot of people are upset with your friend.

_____

Name_____ Date _____

Sharing What Is Important

How are these characters sharing with other people something they feel is important?

1.

Why don't you come to this meeting on creativity with me? You'll learn all kinds of ways to express yourself! It's fun!

_____
_____
_____
_____

2.

I'm going to volunteer to help with the kindergarten soccer team. Those little kids are so cute and they need so much help learning to play! They also need to learn about teamwork!

_____
_____
_____
_____

3.

I love horses and I'd be happy to give you some lessons. Maybe we can trade some riding time with some sailing lessons. What do you think?

_____
_____
_____
_____

4.

I know Josh would like to join us on a bike ride, but he doesn't have a bike. Let him take mine and I'll borrow my brother's. (If I can get that flat tire fixed!)

_____
_____
_____

5.

It would really embarrass Bonnie to wear these jeans if she knew they came from a second-hand store. Let's all go together and pick out jeans from that store. If we all do it, it'll be okay.

_____
_____
_____

6.

Hey, Steve, you need to know that people are starting to talk about you and how you seem to be stoned all the time. I think we should either talk about this or make sure things are under control with you.

_____
_____
_____

Social Skills Applied in the Community
Routine Situations

INSTRUCTOR PAGE

Introduction: As members of a community, we are expected to value and respect our surroundings and the structure that organizes it. These worksheets emphasize the use of basic social skills to get along well in a community.

WORKSHEETS

Note: Answers to the worksheets will vary according to the ages and developmental stages of your students. The answers provided in the Answer Keys are models for typical responses you should expect from your students. As with any other activity, accept answers that can be logically supported by facts.

Worksheet #61: Having Respect for the Property of Others

Answer Key:

1. no; 2. no; 3. no; 4. yes; 5. no; 6. yes

Worksheet #62: Demonstrating Good Manners Towards Others

Answer Key:

1. understanding another's point of view; being a good listener

2. being able to assess a situation; being flexible; controlling emotions

3. using sense of humor; making a good impression

Worksheet #63: Respecting Community Authority Figures

Answer Key:

1. be polite, listen; 2. pay the fine; 3. practice; 4. move on, talk somewhere else; 5. discuss it politely with her; negotiate?; 6. sense of humor; make a good impression; 7. understand another's point of view—company policy; 8. talk to your parents for permission

Worksheet #64: Being Aware of Local Issues

Answer Key:

accidents frequently occurring at a railroad crossing

new recycling center built

teen center being considered

installation of cable TV in new neighborhoods

discussion about raising speed limits on the highway

fund raiser for family whose house burned down

Worksheet #65: Supporting Your Community

Answer Key:

1. join 4-H; 2. sponsor or participate in a walk-a-thon; 3. join sports team; 4. participate in making a float; 5. initiate building a teen center

Name_____ Date _____

Having Respect for the Property of Others

Check (✓) which of these individuals are being good neighbors by showing respect for the property of others.

1. [ ]

Let's carve our names in this tree!

Hey, I've got a better idea. Let's spray paint them on this wall!!

2. [ ]

It's a shortcut to get to the library by cutting across this yard. See? There's already a path. Everyone else does it.

3. [ ]

Are you done with that soda? Just toss the cup out the window. One little piece of trash won't matter.

4. [ ]

It's a real pain to have to carry a little shovel and bag whenever I take Sweetie for a walk. But I guess it could be a problem.

5. [ ]

Let's ride our mountain bikes up the Martinsons' hill. They won't care.

6. [ ]

I wonder if we could play softball in the field next to that huge house. Why don't we ask them first?

Name_____   Date _____

Worksheet #62

Demonstrating Good Manners
Towards Others

Discuss how these people are showing good manners towards others. Write the social skills they are demonstrating.

1.

Good morning, Mrs. Beason. How are you today?

Well, I've got aches and pains all over. My corns and bunions just aren't getting any better. It's awful to be old.

I'm sorry to hear that. Let me know if there's any thing I can do for you!

_____
_____
_____
_____
_____

2.

This guy is driving so fast, he's practically in my back seat!

Wait a minute—I think it's my uncle. He's probably late for his doctor's visit. I'll pull over so he can pass. I'm not in that big of a hurry.

Give him the finger! He shouldn't be on the road!

_____
_____
_____
_____

3.

Boys, your music is just too loud! We can hardly hear ourselves talk at the dinner table.

Oh, sorry about that. We'll try to keep it down.

Thanks. We'd really appreciate it.

No problem. But remember—someday we may be famous musicians and then you'll have to PAY to hear us. Now it's free.

I can wait.

_____
_____
_____
_____
_____

Name_____ Date _____

Respecting Community Authority Figures

How could you respond to authority figures in these situations by demonstrating appropriate social skills?

1. A police officer who pulls you over for running through a stop sign.

   _____

2. The librarian who informs you that your book is overdue and you now have a huge fine to pay.

   _____

3. The driver's education instructor who tells you that your parallel parking is awful and you aren't going to get your license until it improves.

   _____

4. The principal of an elementary school who says that you and your group of friends need to keep moving when you go past the school, not to stand in front and talk, because parents are coming by with cars to pick up their little kids.

   _____

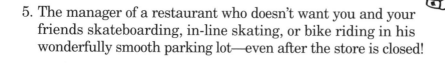

5. The manager of a restaurant who doesn't want you and your friends skateboarding, in-line skating, or bike riding in his wonderfully smooth parking lot—even after the store is closed!

   _____

6. The security guard at the mall who says that only two teenagers are allowed in the stores at a time.

   _____

7. The bank teller who says you have to have two forms of identification to cash a check, even though you have had a checking account at the bank for six months.

   _____

8. The manager of a tanning booth who won't let you tan unless you are over 16 years of age or are there with a parent.

   _____

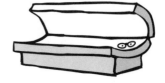

Being Aware of Local Issues

Find out what is going on in your community that concerns you, your peers, your family, and other aspects of your life. Check through your local newspaper or listen to a local radio station. What's important in your community that you need to be aware of? Here are some possibilities:

- recreational places for teens to visit

- rules and regulations for using the beach facilities

- restoring or destroying historic buildings

- school policies for graduation

- youth employment procedures and opportunities

- prices going up at the local retail stores

- community lessons or sports events

- businesses going on strike

- remodeling schools in the community

- road repair

List some other possibilities:

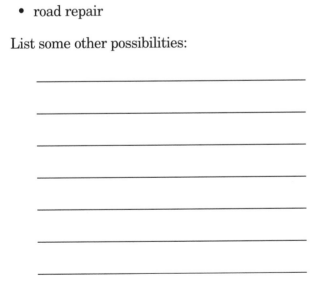

Name_____ Date _____

Supporting Your Community

What are some ways you can become involved in your community? Here are some possibilities.
On the back of this sheet, list some other possibilities.

1.

I'm going to join 4-H. At the fair this summer, I'm going to show the great quilt I made. I used my great-grandmother's old pattern.

_____
_____
_____
_____

2.

The Animal Shelter is in danger of closing. I'm joining a Walk-a-Thon to raise money to keep it open. Care to sponsor me???

_____
_____
_____
_____

3.

We're playing on a co-ed baseball team. We don't care if we win or not; in fact, we'll probably lose every game because we just want to have fun.

_____
_____
_____
_____

4.

We're making a float for the Fourth of July Parade. I'm dressing up as a clown and I'm going to throw candy to all the little kids.

Great! Our float is to promote Good Dental Hygiene!

_____
_____
_____

5.

We wish there was a place where teens could go to have fun without drugs, but with good music and food. We're trying to talk to some local business people to help support our efforts and find a place for us.

_____
_____
_____
_____

Social Skills Applied in the Community
Problems or Unusual Situations

INSTRUCTOR PAGE

Introduction: Things don't always run smoothly in even the quietest community. These worksheets examine ways to function within a community in which there are problems or needs.

WORKSHEETS

Note: Answers to the worksheets will vary according to the ages and developmental stages of your students. The answers provided in the Answer Keys are models for typical responses you should expect from your students. As with any other activity, accept answers that can be logically supported by facts.

Worksheet #66: Dealing With Community Problems

Answer Key:

1. have neighborhood patrols
2. more police involvement
3. install more lights in public places
4. awareness of the problem; focus on community pride
5. keep open minded; keep tempers under control
6. go through proper channels—school board, etc.
7. call for accountability
8. stiffer penalties for abuse
9. higher fines
10. build teen center; have teen nights designated for activities
11. year-round awareness and preparation
12. better enforcement of problem areas
13. health department involved, social service agencies
14. incentives for hiring
15. more funding for needed transportation

Worksheet #67: Improving the Community's Physical Areas

Answer Key:

1. talk to community leaders
2. get a petition circulated
3. find out appropriate location for trails
4. find out estimated cost
5. organize a clean-up day
6. ask for donated materials (paint, brushes, etc.)
7. ask for volunteers
8. put up posters advertising the needed project
9. talk to local farmers to determine interest
10. find out estimated cost of banners
11. organize community Spirit Day at local park

12. community craft fair on Main Street

13. bake sale to benefit needy at Block Party

14. toy donation for Christmas gifts at mall or shopping center

15. decorate town square or courthouse

Worksheet #68: Dealing With Annoying People or Areas

Answer Key:

1. estimate costs, get a petition, put ad in the local paper

2. find out places where dogs are welcome

3. ask for designated picnic areas—no fireworks allowed

4. complain to the manager of the theater

5. put up signs, ask for police patrol periodically through area

6. determine who has priority—biker or pedestrian

Worksheet #69: Creating or Maintaining Safe Places of Leisure

Answer Key:

1. safety checks, police patrol

2. give them your business

3. participate with your group (church, civic, etc.)

4. buy and sell!

5. encourage kids to join, sponsor them, buy products, etc.

6. give some of your time to worthy groups

7. attend activities

8. make sure you can swim, lifeguard on duty

9. adult supervision, no drugs or gangs

10. join a league

11. jogging trail, bike path, horseback riding

12. public beach—maintain, hire a lifeguard

Worksheet #70: Safety in Your Community

Answer Key:

Survey results will vary but should reflect a consensus of what your community is like.

Name_____   Date _____

Worksheet #66 Dealing with Community Problems

Every community has its own set of problems or concerns. You can become involved in making your community a better place, despite the problems it may have. Consider these examples of community problems. Decide to what extent it might affect your own community. If it does, what are some ideas that might help lessen the problem?

1. vandalism, graffiti, shoplifting _____

2. gang violence _____

3. theft of stereo equipment from cars _____

4. racial tension _____

5. businesses going on strike _____

6. problems with the local school system _____

7. distrust of community leaders _____

8. drugs _____

9. speeding _____

10. not enough places for teens to go or things for teens to do

_____

11. seasonal problems, such as flooding of lakes

_____

12. fishing or hunting problems _____

13. overcrowding in apartments or living areas

_____

14. people losing their jobs, businesses closing down

_____

15. inadequate public transportation _____

Name_____ Date _____

Improving the Community's Physical Areas

What are some areas of your community that you think need to be improved? What improvements do you think need to be made? How could you go about taking the first step toward making that improvement?

Ideas

1. creating a new park: _____

2. adding a public swimming pool to an existing park: _____

3. developing bike trails:_____

4. tearing down old houses that are ready to fall down: _____

5. cleaning up a litter-filled field: _____

6. painting some houses in an old neighborhood: _____

7. repairing broken fences: _____

8. planting flowers:_____

9. having a farmer's market on Main Street during the summer:

   _____

10. putting up community banners along the street lights on a main street to advertise upcoming events:

   _____

Other ideas:

11. _____

12. _____

13. _____

14. _____

15. _____

Worksheet #68

Dealing with Annoying People or Areas

How might you respond to people who are not willing to listen to your attempts to make your community a better place?

1. *Sorry kid, it's just not possible to put in a roller rink. It would be too expensive and we don't think enough people would go to make it worthwhile. Sorry.*

_____
_____
_____
_____

2. *You can't walk your dog in the park. Can't you read that sign? You'll have to go somewhere else.*

NO DOGS

_____
_____
_____
_____

3. *Hey, we were here first. Move.*

_____
_____
_____
_____

4. *You just told those people that the movie was sold out, but you let those guys in.*

Well, they are friends of mine.

SOLD OUT

_____
_____
_____

5. *How can we clean up this park when people keep dumping stuff here every day? It's impossible to keep up with it! Who would bother to dump off a COUCH?*

_____
_____
_____
_____

6. *This is a bike path! Get out of the way!*

Hey, walkers can come here, too! Be careful and slow down!

_____
_____
_____

Name_____ Date _____

Creating or Maintaining Safe
Places of Leisure

What places or activities are available in your community for people to go to for fun? How can you help make sure these places stay around for awhile and they remain safe?

Examples

1. amusement park:_____

2. coffee house: _____

3. community festival: _____

4. craft show: _____

5. 4-H Club: _____

6. volunteer groups: _____

7. YMCA activities: _____

8. swimming pool: _____

9. video arcade/pool hall for teens: _____

10. bowling alley: _____

Other examples:

11. _____

12. _____

13. _____

14. _____

15. _____

Safety in the Community

How safe is your community? Create a survey that indicates what concerns you might have about safety. Have several other people (adults, other teens, children) respond to your survey and come to some conclusions.

Examples:

- Do you always lock your car in the school parking lot?

  _____

- Do you always lock your house or apartment?

  _____

- Do you feel safe being out alone after dark in the middle of town?

  _____

- Would you feel safe carrying $100 cash in your purse or wallet?

  _____

- Do you feel like you know your neighbors fairly well?

  _____

- Do you know the name of at least one local police officer?

  _____

- Where would you go if you felt someone was following you?

  _____

- Do you think most people have a gun in their house?

  _____

- What would you do if someone you didn't know came up to your door and asked to use your phone?

  _____

- Do your parents always want to know where you are and have a set time for when you should be in?

  _____

Survey Results: _____

_____

_____

_____

_____

_____

Social Skills Applied in the Community
Enhancing Life in Your Community

INSTRUCTOR PAGE

Introduction: There are many ways to become actively involved in making your community outstanding. If everyone participated, your community could truly be an exceptional place to live. It all begins, however, with one person making a commitment—*you!*

WORKSHEETS

Note: Answers to the worksheets will vary according to the ages and developmental stages of your students. The answers provided in the Answer Keys are models for typical responses you should expect from your students. As with any other activity, accept answers that can be logically supported by facts.

Worksheet #71: Volunteering at Agencies

Answer Key:

1. teaching reading
2. volunteering at a nursing home
3. helping out with the community theater group
4. delivering hot meals to elderly or disabled people

Worksheet #72: Learning About Local Political Groups

Answer Key:

Answers will vary.

Worksheet #73: Organizing Community Activities

Answer Key:

1. building a house for a needy family
2. taking nursing home residents out to lunch
3. redecorating the Community Center
4. adding audio-visual equipment to the public library

Worksheet #74: Getting Involved in Fund-Raising Causes

Answer Key:

1. put up signs around the community
2. run radio and/or TV ads
3. go door-to-door with leaflets about your fund raiser
4. decorate the route of a walk-a-thon
5. wear colored arm bands or ribbons

Worksheet #75: Supporting Efforts to Improve the Community

Answer Key:

Answers will vary.

Name_____ Date _____

Volunteering at Agencies

How have these individuals helped to contribute to make their community better by volunteering?

1.

Ready to read? We're up to lesson 15 this week.

I sure appreciate your help. I wish I could read better.

_____

_____

_____

_____

2.

Is there anything I can get for you?

Just help me write a letter to my daughter. She lives so far away and I don't get to see her very often.

_____

_____

_____

_____

3.

It's only two weeks until our community play!

Let's paint a huge sign and hang it up in front of the courthouse so everyone will see it and come!!

_____

_____

_____

_____

4.

Here's a list of older or disabled people who need meals delivered.

We're on our way!

_____

_____

_____

_____

Learning About Local Political Groups

Find out who your local leaders are and what their plans are for your community. You might want to select one (or two) and conduct an interview to find out more.

Where to start:

- members of your local school board

- the mayor of your town

- business leaders

- political party headquarters

- people who work in the community courthouse

- local police department

- people in the news—who and why?

- parks and recreation departments

Others:

- _____

- _____

- _____

- _____

- _____

- _____

- _____

- _____

Notes:

_____

_____

_____

_____

_____

_____

_____

_____

_____

_____

_____

_____

Worksheet #73 **Organizing Community Activities**

How could you get involved in organizing some community activities? Select an activity or two and decide how you might go about becoming more involved. Here's an example.

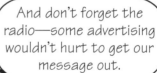

Name_____ Date _____

Getting Involved in
Fund-Raising Causes

From time to time, communities sponsor fund-raising activities to help local people or situations. Consider how you could become involved in something like this:

- a roller-skating party to benefit Brady, who has leukemia

  _____

- a bake sale to benefit people who were hurt in a boiler accident

  _____

- a car wash to help send some fifth graders to London for a student exchange program in the summer

  _____

- a walkathon to help raise money for a new animal shelter

  _____

- selling chocolate candy bars to raise money for new band uniforms

  _____

- rent-a-student for odd jobs to help raise money for the Spanish club to go to Mexico for a week

  _____

- posters and money canisters placed in local businesses to create awareness of a family whose home was destroyed by fire

  _____

- a huge thermometer showing the amount of money raised toward the community goal for a specific purpose

  _____

  _____

  _____

Name_____ Date _____

Supporting Efforts to Improve the Community

What are some ways your community is taking steps to make improvements? How can you be a part of it? Here are some examples.

1.

We need a railroad crossing sign and lights at the highway. There have been too many accidents there.

2.

We're having a Cruise Night this summer in July. We're asking everyone to clear the main route through town for a few hours so the old cars can go through on parade.

3.

The speed limit in front of the school is not being followed by anyone. Drivers are going too fast down that road. We need to post a lower limit. I know this will be unpopular, but we've got a lot of little kids who walk to school.

4.

The new mall just opened. I try to do my shopping locally to give my business to the local merchants.

5.

If we want this beach to stay open, we need to make sure we follow the rules. No littering, stay within the ropes, etc. Hey . . . I wonder if we could add a snack bar!